ALSO BY DOUG SMITH

Airborne

WE THE NORTH

25 Years of the Toronto Raptors

Doug Smith

VIKING

VIKING

an imprint of Penguin Canada, a division of Penguin Random House Canada Limited

Canada • USA • UK • Ireland • Australia • New Zealand • India • South Africa • China

First published 2020

www.penguinrandomhouse.ca

Library and Archives Canada Cataloguing in Publication

Title: We the North : 25 years of the Toronto Raptors / Doug Smith.
Names: Smith, Doug, 1958– author.
Identifiers: Canadiana (print) 20200175920 | Canadiana (ebook) 20200175939 | ISBN 9780735240360 (hardcover) | ISBN 9780735240377 (HTML)
Subjects: LCSH: Toronto Raptors (Basketball team)—History.
Classification: LCC GV885.52.T67 S66 2020 | DDC 796.323/6409713541—dc23

Cover and book design: Terri Nimmo
Cover image: Happy_vector/Getty Images

Printed and bound in the U.S.A.

10 9 8 7 6 5 4 3 2 1

Penguin
Random House
VIKING CANADA

To Susan and Jacob,
for your constant love and support.

CONTENTS

FOREWORD

by Vince Carter

It was a head-scratcher on draft night in 1998 when my North Carolina Tar Heel teammate Antawn Jamison was selected fourth overall by the Toronto Raptors. I knew he hadn't worked out for them, so it didn't make any sense. Before I had a chance to even figure out what was going on, my name was called and I was walking up to the stage to shake commissioner David Stern's hand. I had been drafted by the Golden State Warriors.

As I was talking about my draft-day photo with Stern on stage, he told me to wait because there was going to be a trade. Antawn was going to the Warriors. I was going to the Raptors. Just like that, I was going from the West Coast to Canada in a matter of five minutes.

I had worked out with the Raptors, but outside of the two days I spent there for draft workouts, I knew nothing about Toronto. Immediately after the trade happened, I talked to Tracy McGrady on draft night. Just the year before, T-Mac and I found out we were cousins. Now, we were professional teammates.

The lockout hit after the draft and I didn't arrive in Toronto until January. The first day I landed, I was walking through a blizzard. I was like, *What in the world?* I'm a Florida kid, now coming to a place where it was unbelievably cold. Coming from Chapel Hill, one of the meccas for college basketball, to where we were second fiddle to the Toronto Maple Leafs, which, no pun intended, were the big stick in the city.

We were trying to make our way, to teach the fans the game, and we gave the fans something to be excited about. Oh, by the way, what else do I remember about Toronto? Extra-friendly people. Everyone was just super friendly.

At the time, I had no idea what influence we would have on basketball in Canada. I was a young guy, playing with my cousin, and we were just having fun and enjoying the moment. At one point, I'm not going to lie, T-Mac and I had it on lock. We were out there trying to embarrass and dunk on people. I was young. I didn't understand the impact I was having on the young five- or six-year-old who was attending a Raptors game. I had no clue.

Social media wasn't a thing. You definitely didn't know how much of an impact you had. Now, you can just look at your feed, your mentions, and you can see the impact. The jerseys. The videos of kids re-enacting your dunk. We didn't get an opportunity to see that.

I still remember the day I found out I was traded by the Raptors. It was a weird day. I was in Indiana and woke up from a nap after morning shootaround to a bunch of messages on my phone telling me I had been traded. Then I was sitting with Alvin Williams, Jalen Rose, and Milt Palacio. We said our goodbyes before they went to the arena for the game. I was sitting in my hotel not knowing how to feel. I didn't know how to handle it.

Looking back on it, it was tough. The toughest thing to handle was that people questioned my love for the city of Toronto and the game. It was tough at the time to tell my side or to prove to people. It just had to organically happen over time. I believe that time heals all wounds. Once people gained more knowledge of the situation, it helped smooth things over.

I always wanted people to know that the night I was traded, the next day, and the days after that, I didn't have any ill feelings over the team and the city. I loved the city. It's unfortunate whoever put that out there. They were so far wrong. I remember Doug Smith wanted to have a feature conversation about all of that at the time, to shed some light on the actual situation, but it just wasn't the right time. And I understood that.

So did Doug. It probably sounds weird to say this because a lot of athletes and media aren't really *one* with each other all the time, but Doug was a guy I gravitated to over the years. I got to know him, and through having conversations with him, we developed a trust. Even after I moved on from Toronto, we kept in touch, and through all the ugliness of my departure from the Raptors, we talked. Doug understood me as well as my teammates did.

That's rare in sports. For athletes, trust is always tough, and trusting the media is even more of a sensitive fine line. But over our six years together in Toronto, we became friends. Doug understood my ups and downs, he understood my moods, and we approached each other with respect and in the right way. Maybe I'm biased because I've gotten to know him over the years, but I know that the things I say will be the things that come out, and they're in good hands when I say them to Doug.

Flash forward to June 2019. I was in Toronto again for a playoff game for the first time since I played in a Raptors jersey. It was

Game 5 of the NBA finals. I was sitting with T-Mac. It was insane. I had chills that night. The Raptors lost, but I remember sitting there after the game and telling T-Mac, "Imagine if they win the championship, how crazy would that be?"

I was in Oakland for Game 6. The evening the Raptors clinched their first NBA championship. It was unbelievable. In the second half, I looked at T-Mac and we were like, *They are really about to win the championship.* The Toronto Raptors. This team we played for so many years ago.

It was a proud moment for me to witness it and be in the building for it. To see my good friend Kyle Lowry and people in the Raptors organization who I still know, I was so happy for all of them. To leave the arena, we had to walk through the court after the game. I gave Kyle a big hug and congratulated him. I saw my friend superfan Nav Bhatia, who was on another level on the court.

It was awesome to see all the Raptors fans celebrating. I was happy to be there just to witness it, just to say that I was there. It was a special moment.

For me, it was a way to bring it all full circle.

Vince Carter
April 2020

INTRODUCTION

It's hard to think of how many times over the last 25 years something has happened with the Raptors, good or bad, last year or in 1995, when I've thought, "Man, that's one for the book."

Well, here it is.

It's hard for me to imagine how we got to this point, how I've become so ingrained with one sports franchise that enough stories have been amassed and enough history has been witnessed that I could come up with these recollections, opinions, and thoughts.

Incredible, really.

The ride has been tumultuous and enthralling and all-encompassing for a quarter of a century. It's taken me all over the world, allowed me to see feats of athleticism up close that have at times been breathtaking. It's allowed me to meet and get to know some incredible men and women, masters of sports and of business, fascinating personalities I got to interact with every single day of my professional life for longer than most.

I know Wayne Embry and Masai Ujiri because I cover the Raptors, I count Dwane Casey and Sam Mitchell and Brendan Malone as friends.

I watched Vince Carter up close and I saw Kawhi Leonard's steely determination end with a raucous championship celebration.

I sipped wine in Treviso with Maurizio Gherardini and got Madrid restaurant recommendations from Jorge Garbajosa.

Thanks to the Raptors and the NBA and basketball, I've been to eight Summer Olympics, four World Championships, and more NBA finals than I can remember. Games in Honolulu and Rome and Madrid and London.

All because I wanted to write about basketball in 1994 when no one else did.

An incredible ride.

There were bumps and fun moments and sad moments. I saw good friends lose their jobs and far too many dreary losses to count, and the night I got hit square in the eyeglasses by a T-shirt fired out of a T-shirt cannon by the mascot of the Denver Nuggets during a pre-season game in Colorado Springs should have turned me off the game and its extraneous crap forever.

But it didn't. None of it did. I loved the game, I appreciated the job, I did it 100 percent full out because that's what it deserved.

In some weird way, I owe the Raptors my life.

If not for team doctors Paul Marks and Howard Petroff, head athletic trainer Scott McCullough, and a physician friend of Larry Tanenbaum who was just enjoying a night at a game one Sunday evening in 2016, I would not be here to write this.

They, and my great dear friend Jennifer Quinn, saved my life after I collapsed with an aortic dissection in the hallway outside the Directors Lounge of what's now known as the Scotiabank Arena.

Prompt medical attention, a shot of nitroglycerin, and much comfort kept me going until the fine doctors and nurses at the

Munk Cardiac Centre at Toronto General Hospital got me back to full health.

That's being tied to a franchise, isn't it?

When Nick Garrison of Penguin Random House first approached me about this project, we wondered just what "the story" was going to be because simply retelling the tale of a championship season was too narrow a focus.

It is, I thought, more a story of the evolution of a sport and, more important, a society. I said that when I looked out over the crowds that jammed the streets of Toronto, and of Canada, to watch the Raptors in the playoffs the last few years, the people I saw far more reflected the country in which we live than any crowd at any other sporting event in Canada.

White, black, brown.

Male, female, transgender, non-binary.

Old, young, somewhere in between.

Rich and poor, famous and anonymous.

That was the crowd and that was my Canada.

It has been the tale of the franchise as well. As I've tried to show in the pages to come, the story of the Raptors is not only the story of the evolution of a sport and a team but of a fan base, a society, a country.

Over all these years, it has been my great pleasure, my great honour, and my great responsibility to tell that story. Good stories, bad stories, happy stories and sad ones, it's been a helluva ride from 1995 to now.

We've all grown because of it—and are better off for having been around it.

I hope you've enjoyed the ride as much as I have.

1

FIRST GAME

The first Toronto Raptors game was always going to be emotional for me. I grew up in Niagara Falls and would occasionally go watch the Buffalo Braves play at the old Aud, a relic of a barn with a vertigo-inducing upper deck. It was the time of Bob McAdoo and the criminally underrated Randy Smith, Dr. Jack Ramsay on the bench, Ernie DiGregorio, and those baby blue uniforms. The college scene in the area focused on the Little Three—Niagara University, St. Bonaventure, and Canisius—Calvin Murphy, Bob Lanier, and coach Frank Layden.

In high school, I played baseball together with Jay Triano, who would go on to be Team Canada's men's basketball head coach. We competed against each other in basketball and watched a series of local heroes play from Stamford Collegiate, the old alma mater.

I played for Niagara College while learning how to be a journalist, and let's just say the mighty Knights were not a dominant force among Ontario College Athletic Association squads. How would I describe my own game? I was the heady point guard. The most athletic? Certainly not. But I was the brain trust. We had one go-to play, the pick and roll, and it didn't really work that well too many times.

But the game somehow got into my blood. I wasn't particularly good at it but it was good for me; I could see the teamwork, the ballet-like unison needed to be successful, the athleticism that wasn't near the level of today but that was impressive for the times. Hell, in the mid-1970s in the Niagara Peninsula, the measure of your game wasn't if you could dunk—you had hops if you could touch the rim. Different times, indeed.

Flash forward to 1991, which was when I started working for the Canadian Press. When it was announced that Toronto would get an NBA franchise a couple of years later, the wire service needed a basketball guy and I was going to be that guy. I'd done baseball when the Blue Jays were good, covering both the 1992 and 1993 World Series championships, and had covered the 1991 Toronto Argonauts of Rocket Ismail, Wayne Gretzky, John Candy, and Bruce McNall. Time for a change.

That was a different time, before basketball became as much the fabric of sports in Toronto as hockey and other major professional sports. If you can believe it, nobody really cared about the basketball-beat writer gig. The Blue Jays had just recently won back-to-back World Series. The Leafs? They came close a few times, but regardless of the results, they were the Leafs. Everybody wanted to write about hockey.

Covering basketball in Toronto? It wasn't necessarily the most stable job to take. A lot of people were skeptical as to whether this whole basketball-in-Toronto thing was even going to last. Just a year before the Raptors started playing, this city hosted the 1994 FIBA World Championship. This wasn't the United States' original Dream

Team of 1992, when Michael Jordan, Larry Bird, and Magic Johnson roamed the streets of Barcelona and Charles Barkley became an international rock star.

But still, there was star power. I still remember being at a bar one night on Front Street drinking with the coaching staff of the Russian team. Even if just for a few weeks, basketball had taken over the city of Toronto. Team Canada wasn't particularly good. They had a game at Maple Leaf Gardens against Greece. The winner would move past the round robin. The crowd was 85 percent cheering for Greece. Boy, were the Team Canada officials pissed. Rick Fox slipped and missed a shot at the buzzer. The home team lost. Team Canada would finish in ninth.

But this provided a glimpse of what was possible for basketball in Toronto. You had the international community and a chance to win over the younger and more diverse sports fans in the city, the people who didn't live and die by the Toronto Maple Leafs. It was no coincidence why the brain trust of John Bitove and Isiah Thomas looked to some international players—Vincenzo Esposito, Žan Tabak—on that very first team. Toronto was changing and Canada was changing, thanks to the global impact of the Dream Team at the 1992 Barcelona Olympics, and there truly was an untapped market out there. It was prescient to cater to it, but vitally important as the city, the country, and the game evolved.

As for the name and those cartoony jerseys? They were mocked at the time—who wore pinstripes in basketball?—but a quarter of a century later, they're fun to see, lovable almost, and when the 2020 version of the Raptors brought back the white ones, they were all the rage. Hell, Kyle Lowry wearing a white pinstriped Damon Stoudamire throwback during the 2019 championship parade was an iconic moment. I was too old to understand the references to *Jurassic Park*. I didn't know what the hell it meant. Of course it was gimmicky, maybe tacky even. But the Raptors needed gimmicks to help them. I understood the cartoon nature. People made fun of it. Fans of opposing teams made fun of them, opposing players mocked them. The team would be introduced on the road to *Barney* theme music in later years. I didn't really care, then or now, but I was neither wearing the jerseys nor the target audience for them.

They appealed to the younger kids in the city, who would ask their parents if they could have a Raptors T-shirt or get a pair of $5 tickets to sit in the 500 level at the SkyDome to watch their favourite team play. If the kids liked that goofy little dinosaur on the jersey, what did it matter what this beat writer thought?

Everything about that first season was new. I still remember the very first pre-season game. It was played in Halifax at what was known then as the Civic Centre. The Raptors played the Philadelphia 76ers. Two writers from Philadelphia had made the trip: Phil Jasner and Joe Juliano, two veteran NBA writers who were venturing to Canada to cover a game for the first time. They drove to the airport together after the game. The two teams were playing again in Saint John. On the way there, the two realized they had booked a flight to St. John's, Newfoundland. The game was gonna be in Saint John, New Brunswick.

Basketball in Canada. It was new for everyone. There was going to be an adjustment period for all of us. The Raptors even played for a trophy in their first pre-season. Can you imagine, two NBA teams competing for a trophy before they even played their first official game? But this really happened. It was the Naismith Cup in Winnipeg. The trophy is named after the man who invented the sport, and the game between the Raptors and the Vancouver Grizzlies was hyped as the battle for NBA supremacy in the country.

I wonder how James Naismith would've felt if he'd watched this game. The Raptors won—they always seemed to beat Vancouver—and they wheeled out this 10-foot-long table, put it at mid-court, and brought out the trophy. It was the size of a laptop. Talk about underwhelming. This tiny little thing. That's what they were playing for. Tony Massenburg hurt himself for nothing, one of the few recognizable names on the Raptors roster gone for months because of an injury that occurred in some inconsequential pre-season game.

Nowadays, the Raptors have one of the most knowledgeable fan bases in the NBA. Back then, there was a lot of educating going on, whether it was on the broadcast or through the media. When the FIBA Championship happened in 1994, Hubie Brown, a legendary NBA coach who went on to be a revered broadcaster, came and conducted a media training session with the reporters.

I'm talking about rudimentary basketball knowledge. "The court is 94 feet" type stuff. I left that session. I couldn't do it. To be honest, as someone who grew up watching basketball, it felt very condescending. But that came with the territory. Everybody was learning. Everybody was new.

There were a lot of people in the media who needed those lessons. The illegal defence rules were very convoluted. Thankfully, Brendan Malone, the very first Raptors head coach, would make time to explain some of these intricacies. I knew about the 94 feet of the court, but some of the other stuff that Malone explained did help me. It helped a lot of guys. We knew the rules. We knew the players. But there was a learning curve. And it was so steep that there were those among us who totally disregarded basketball in search of a story.

The very first game that actually counted would be played at the SkyDome against the New Jersey Nets. Four hours before tipoff on opening night, team officials were bolting in seats on the temporary stands. You have to understand, this wasn't a stadium built for basketball. The court was in right field, and it ran from the right field foul line to centre field.

Dinner was upstairs where the baseball press box was. There was a work area for media on the court, and it was curtained off in the back. After games, the front-end loaders would use machinery to tear down the temporary stands. It was noise you had to work around. The quirks of being in a baseball stadium for a basketball game.

I'll never forget so many moments about that first game on November 3, 1995. I was sitting in my press box when I watched Alvin Robertson, at that time a nine-year NBA veteran who had the most impressive résumé of any player on the roster, walk across the stadium from left field, crossing the infield into the locker room to get ready for his first game as a Raptor. He'll go down in history as the player to score the very first Raptors points. Forgotten now is that he almost didn't even play in the first game.

John Lashway, the very first Toronto Raptors PR guy, had gotten a call from the police at 2:30 a.m. the night before. Robertson had been arrested for allegedly assaulting a woman in the SkyDome hotel lobby. Bail was secured—although charges were later dismissed when the complainant decided not to testify. Then he scored the first basket in franchise history, a jumpshot right in front of the Raptors bench, and finished with 30 points. Today, his arrest would be the main story. Back then, it was like the fourth paragraph. Different times, indeed.

It was an inauspicious start for the franchise.

But the first game was a very emotional experience for me and a lot of people in the stadium that night. The 1995 Quebec referendum had happened only four days earlier; before that date, it was touch and go as to whether the Canada we knew and loved would even exist, and the fact that Quebec remained in Canada after a 51–49 percent voting split told the story of a nation with issues to resolve. So when the Barenaked Ladies came out to sing the national anthems on opening night and broke into French during the Canadian anthem, everyone cheered. It was an emotional scene.

But it was also a celebration of sorts. The Raptor—the most enduring mascot in the NBA—was "born" by breaking out of a giant egg, an over-the-top moment that went with the over-the-top mood of the night, public address announcer Herbie Kuhn insinuating himself into the action as so many do, something no Toronto sports fan had ever experienced. That both of them are still in their roles a quarter of a century later is stunning, but it does prove that the original Raptors organization got it right. They were and are entertaining, staples of the experience of attending a Raptors game even to this day, and I don't think any of us in the building that night would have seen that coming.

The SkyDome packed a lot of people into the building, which was good. You could pay $5 to be in the arena to watch an NBA game and see superstars you only ever saw on TV or read about in the newspaper, although good luck to you being able to see much of the on-court action. Thankfully, there was a jumbotron. The Dome was such a cavernous building. It was hard to deliver an intimate viewing experience, and to me, basketball should be intimate. It was painful watching 41 games a season in that place. It was too big because one of the most alluring aspects of live basketball is its intimacy, and that was impossible to capture in a cavernous facility that could hold 50,000 fans. The sound was lost as it travelled up to the roof, the scoreboards were temporary as were half the stands, and fans in the upper deck were so far removed from the game they may as well have stayed in the comfort of their homes. The games were fun a lot of times that season but it was in spite of the facility, not because of it.

The first game was filled with excitement. Robertson scored the first points. The Raptors raced out to a lead. They were winning quite comfortably. And then there was the entertainment aspect. That was important to the Raptors, too.

"In the first game [of the season], it was like an extravaganza before the game. We had all kinds of people parading around with costumes on, and then we went out and I'm thinking, 'Are we going to win a game this season?' And we went out and we beat New Jersey handily," coach Brendan Malone once said of that historic night. "I think Toronto fell in love with that team."

There was this Bleacher Creature guy. He would show up in the 500 levels and egg all the people up to the top to cheer the Raptors on. He had a knack for getting people excited but mostly because no Toronto sports fan had ever seen anything like it.

The mascot did mascot things like jumping off a mini-trampoline and dunking basketballs while the fans roared. He'd goof around with the fans and in the crowd—a pratfall here, a hug for a kid there—all things that were new to the city. The Dance Pak was a new idea, and to the team's everlasting credit, the very first version included men and women and how forward-thinking was that? It was truly unlike any other sporting experience in Toronto at the time.

Remember what I said about this being a learning experience for everybody? The first game was part of that process. The Raptors had a mix-up and somehow gave out thundersticks to the wrong end of the court. Imagine the players' confusion when they saw a bunch of their own fans waving thundersticks at them to distract them from making free throws.

I don't blame anyone, though. That was probably the first time anyone in Toronto saw a thunderstick in a game.

Theatrics and emotions aside, there was a basketball game at hand. And the Raptors would win comfortably. The Toronto Raptors were officially in the NBA record books. They were 1–0.

Leaving the stadium that evening, there was a sense that basketball in Toronto had finally arrived. I always thought basketball would work here. But seeing it in person, it was like, okay, this is real now.

Everyone—from the front office to the players to the staff to all the people who had a hand in pulling off that first game—was proud, and probably relieved. It had been a long journey to get to that point.

Now, there were 81 games left. The first one was out of the way. The theatrics of the inaugural game would give way to the grind of a long regular season for a roster of players cobbled together from many different franchises.

If they were to succeed on the court, though, they would have to count on their rookie point guard to lead them. Damon Stoudamire started that very first game and went on to play 38 minutes with 10 points and 10 assists. Those were hardly earth-shattering statistics, and his game that night is lost in the memory banks filled with so many other points of reference. But it was one of the few games that entire season where he wasn't the focal point, because as fans new to basketball and the NBA would soon come to know, it's a star-driven game.

And Damon Stoudamire, Mighty Mouse, was truly the team's first star.

2

DAMON STOUDAMIRE

On the morning of the 1995 NBA draft held at the SkyDome in Toronto, the Toronto Raptors, who held the seventh overall pick in the draft, called a five-foot guard from the University of Arizona in for a second workout.

None of us knew about that until later that night, long after history had been made with the franchise's very first draft pick, but looking back, none of us should have been the least bit surprised.

When you're an expansion team like the Raptors, the odds are stacked against you to succeed. You pay what at the time was an astonishing amount—$125 million US—to join the league, and then you're rewarded by a bunch of restrictions. You better get it right, or as right as you possibly can, given the rules stacked against you.

In the expansion draft, you can pick from a list of about a hundred players the opposing teams choose to not protect, so, end-of-the-roster guys or bloated contracts that nobody wants. That's why no-names, has-beens, and never-was guys like Cuban Andrés Guibert, Dontonio Wingfield, Keith "Mister" Jennings, and this four-year guy plucked from the roster of the Dallas Mavericks by the name of Doug Smith—yeah, honest, a namesake!—ended up on the roster after that June 24 expansion draft that preceded the college draft by one day.

Half the players chosen never even got to Toronto; they were traded or waived or retired before they had to show up, and that put an even greater emphasis on the two-round college draft.

Besides, as part of the expansion agreement, the Raptors and the Vancouver Grizzlies weren't even allowed to get the number-one pick, which left Toronto with the seventh selection after Vancouver chose sixth. Because the roster would be filled out with castoffs, drafting the right guy was imperative.

The Raptors had their sights set on Damon Stoudamire. In his senior season at Arizona, Stoudamire averaged 22.8 points and 7.3 assists. One common thread that has been woven into the fabric of this franchise is its "chip on a shoulder" attitude, an "I'll show you" attitude, so Stoudamire being the first draft pick of the Raptors franchise was very fitting.

The undersized, left-handed, four-year collegian was disregarded by many. But his first workout had gone well, and on the morning of the draft, Isiah Thomas got another look at Stoudamire at a second workout and was convinced. That's when it was decided: the Raptors would be selecting Stoudamire.

The draft was an event, the first time it had ever been held outside the United States, and the Raptors wanted to put on a show. A massive stage for team representatives, a back-of-house area for players and their families to wait, about 20,000 fans in attendance to witness history.

It was a show, indeed.

As the home crowd watched commissioner David Stern announce Toronto's pick, the crowd rained down with boos. Meanwhile, I watched as team owner John Bitove sat on stage, right behind Stern, and cheered as if it was some huge surprise to him. It was all for show. It was odd. But it was part of Bitove's showmanship.

The rest of the stadium wanted Ed O'Bannon. He was the national college player of the year at UCLA. Casual basketball fans watched the March Madness tournament and saw O'Bannon lead the Bruins to the national championship. Fans saw him as the franchise saviour, the obvious pick in the draft. And they reacted accordingly.

The boos were a bit overreactive. I didn't know much about Stoudamire at the time. His Arizona team was a number two seed in the tournament and was upset by Steve Nash's Santa Clara team. Despite that, I remember Nash telling me: "This guy is going to be a player."

I saw the confidence in him even on draft night. Stoudamire wasn't bothered by the boos. He told us: "Wait until these fans watch me play. Trust me, they won't boo me anymore." Strong words, but he backed them up.

Stoudamire was incredible during his first year with the Raptors, exactly the type of guy you wanted to start building your team from scratch.

He was fascinating to watch. He'd go on to remind me of Allen Iverson, another franchise point guard who would join the league as the number-one overall pick the year after. Stoudamire was fearless; he was short, but he could shoot. And he was a perfect young leader on a team of veterans. The vets loved him because of how much Stoudamire cared. He knew he was going to be a rookie and would have to defer to the veterans at some point, but he was also in a weird spot where he was going to be the face of the franchise.

Stoudamire wasn't forceful with the older guys on the team when he led, and the older guys respected that. Besides, a lot of these expansion team guys needed a second chance, and being on the right side of Biggie, as he was known to his teammates, would be good for their NBA careers. There was no doubt where he fit in the pecking order: he was going to be The Guy. Figure it out: an undersized point guard playing for a team whose president was one of the greatest undersized point guards in the history of basketball? Yeah, Isiah Thomas's first draft pick was anointed from the very first night.

The fans grew to love him quickly. One of his memorable performances came early in the season. I still remember the national television game broadcast on TNT at the SkyDome against the Seattle Supersonics. Back then, every team had to appear on TNT at least once a season. Well, they decided to get the expansion team Raptors out of the way early, featuring them in a game against the Gary Payton/Shawn Kemp–led Sonics.

Stoudamire had a triple-double, 20 points, 11 assists, and 12 rebounds, and held his own against Payton, the best defensive point guard in the league. The Raptors won 102–97. It was one of the most shining moments in Stoudamire's Toronto career.

The boos on draft night were quickly forgotten. The fans absolutely loved him. There's something about plucky underdogs, like Doug Gilmour or Doug Flutie, in Canadian sports that draws people to them. Stoudamire fit the billing to a tee.

There was a whole marketing campaign for him, too. Stoudamire became known as the Mighty Mouse. It was the first time we had seen that kind of public marketing campaign for a player. You never saw this kind of push for an individual player on the Toronto Maple Leafs. It made people pay attention, and they loved Mighty Mouse.

It reached its apex that first year with the memorable win over the Chicago Bulls and Michael Jordan in March 1996. The Bulls would ultimately finish with a 72–10 win-loss record while the Raptors would finish 22–60, but somehow the upstart expansion franchise won the game and Stoudamire was a star. With more than 36,000 fans in the stands, Mighty Mouse made six three-point field goals, scored 30 points, and gave the Bulls fits. The Raptors fans loved him before; they really loved him after.

And rivals noticed.

"We just didn't have anybody to stop him," said Steve Kerr, a guard on the Bulls that afternoon and eventually the highly regarded coach of the Golden State Warriors. "He stoned Michael and he stoned me. Most guys with his speed can't shoot."

Even though he had the marketing campaign and was doing well on the court, I'm not entirely sure whether Stoudamire, who was 22 years old at the time, was totally ready to be what the Raptors needed him to be. He wasn't particularly personable. It wasn't because he was an asshole. He just wouldn't go out of his way to make you feel comfortable around him.

Stoudamire would answer our questions, he would do the marketing ads, but he didn't ever seem to do them willingly. I remember interviewing Stoudamire for a book I wrote about him. We were at Lone Star Grill on Front Street in downtown Toronto, and people would come up to our table and ask Stoudamire for a photo, an autograph, or just to chat, and I could tell he didn't really appreciate people bothering him.

It wasn't that he was a bad guy; he was a private guy and he wanted to be able to keep to himself. He'd have shields—he had a buddy who went everywhere with him who would dissuade the general public from being too intrusive with a harsh look or a sharp word—and Damon never liked being bugged in public. He just didn't care for the adulation even though he'd earned it.

I remember thinking at the time, "You are Damon Stoudamire, you are the face of the franchise, you have to handle the public spotlight a little better." But make no mistake, Stoudamire was a good kid. He was young, he liked to have fun away from the game. He'd go out nights and he'd find ways to get in his social recreation, but there always seemed to be a barrier he'd put up. And he enjoyed recreational pursuits that were best handled privately, like so many other 20-something young men and women at the time. And it was not at all just an NBA or athlete thing—if the recreational use of cannabis was a way to unwind, well, unwind they would.

On the court, he was proving people wrong. Isiah Thomas had a bit of an "I told you so" attitude about the whole thing. Thomas saw a lot of himself in Stoudamire. This was an undersized, hard player, a smart player. Thomas was probably more flashy than Stoudamire. But I think they saw a lot in each other. It was a perfect relationship. Stoudamire saw what Thomas had gone through with the Detroit Pistons to win two championships and an NBA finals MVP.

In the second season, the Raptors took Marcus Camby, a centre from UMass. Stoudamire really liked playing with Camby. A big man who could rebound and finish around the basket took a lot of pressure off Stoudamire. I think he also saw the possibilities on the court with Camby. They could have been the one-two combo that would get the Raptors to the playoffs one day.

The two really got along as guys and were good teammates with each other. Camby was an easygoing guy, he got along with everyone. By the third season, the Raptors had taken a teenager named Tracy McGrady, and it appeared a core was in place.

Things fell apart quickly. Front office drama forced Thomas to leave the organization, and Stoudamire, after losing his mentor, put a trade request to interim general manager Glen Grunwald. The thing I remember about Stoudamire is that disastrous third season when they went 16–66; no matter the losing or the trade request, he kept playing hard.

I remember the Raptors went into Los Angeles with a 1–15 record to take on the Lakers. They fought hard, but lost by six. Stoudamire didn't have a good game. He shot 2 for 13. I remember walking to the locker room to ask him about the losing streak they were on. And he just had nothing to say. I walked towards his locker, and he just looked up at me and was almost in tears.

"I got fucking nothing for you, Doug," Stoudamire told me.

He was never standoffish, but Stoudamire took every loss really hard. And the Raptors lost a lot. And the franchise had lost the guy who drafted him. He was heading to free agency. He was beaten down by the losing because he really cared.

Some guys don't try as hard when they make a trade request. That wasn't Stoudamire. It just wasn't in his DNA. He was wired to play hard. None of us knew about the trade request. After Thomas left, we had an inkling that Stoudamire might not have been long for the Raptors. But Grunwald operated very quietly. He kept the trade request private as well.

The trade—February 13, 1998—came when I was in Nagano, covering the Winter Olympics for the *Toronto Star*, and its scope surprised even me. It struck me immediately as an overall loss for the Raptors; they were giving up their very best player, and that was a major, major sea change in the franchise's path.

But the other immediate reaction was that it was good for Stoudamire. He was going home. It was good for him to get a fresh start with a winning team. He got to play with Arvydas Sabonis and make the Western Conference finals and make tons of money.

The Raptors lost that trade. They sent their best player out and got a bunch of guys back, and none of them were good at that time, although we eventually saw what Alvin Williams meant to the Raptors. The season was in the toilet. They finished with 16 wins, and now their promising point guard of the future was gone. It's funny. After all these years, when I look back on Stoudamire, even though he was only here for a brief time, he went on to touch the franchise in so many tiny ways. He was in Memphis when Kyle Lowry was a rookie there. He was a former teammate of Marc Gasol. To this day, he tells me every time we speak that he wishes things had turned out differently, that he and Isiah Thomas could have been together for longer with the Raptors.

He loves the city still—he has recruited high school players from Toronto in his role as the head coach at the University of the Pacific—and it was nice to see him feted by the organization and the fans during Game 1 of the 2019 NBA finals at the Scotiabank Arena.

"I've seen it called an expansion situation but let's get it what it was: an experimental situation because no one knew if it would work," he told me shortly before that night. "It's amazing to see what it is now. I'm proud of what we did."

For the Raptors, though, it was time to move on. The key piece returning in the trade was Kenny Anderson. He was a pretty good player, but he was not in Stoudamire's class at the time, and besides, Damon was "ours" in many ways and there was no one who could replace him in the hearts of fans. And as a gut punch, Anderson decided he wasn't going to report to Toronto. It was an insult to the organization but also to the city. He never spent a day in Toronto. He shipped to Boston in a package deal that centred on this young kid named Chauncey Billups to cap the flurry of trades near the end of a disastrous season.

We were naive enough to think ownership and management ran basketball teams. But this was the first time we realized how much power the players had. A franchise point guard was gone, and it was unclear where the Raptors would go from here.

3

CANADA ISSUES

If you hear NBA players from the United States tell it, you would think living in Canada was akin to being sent off to a faraway place, completely disconnected from your family, without access to your previous life, completely buried under a constant snowstorm in the winter. Really, not much different from entering witness protection, with the exception of the fact that you could still make millions of dollars playing a sport you love and people will still know who you are.

This has been a conversation about the Raptors since they entered the league. The gap between the *perception* of playing for Toronto and the *reality* of playing for Toronto has closed in recent years, but the gripes remain. Kenny Anderson was the first player to publicly reject the notion of moving to Canada to play basketball; others have been skeptical in the years since.

But how many of their complaints result from these players simply not educating themselves on things? Take, for example, a very common complaint: playing in Toronto means it takes hours to clear customs every time you fly from the United States into Canada after a game. This has become a thing. Talk about perception versus reality.

It was December 30, 1999. The Raptors had played in Dallas, and I was supposed to fly back home the next day through Chicago. But remember, this was Y2K; nobody knew what was going to happen when the clock struck midnight on January 1 and the year 2000 arrived. I kid you not, we really thought planes were going to drop out of the sky, so head coach Butch Carter told the other reporters and me that we could fly with them on the team's chartered plane.

Here's the customs process that everyone complains about and has been passed around the league to become a go-to reason no one wants to play in Toronto. Back in those days, before the advance of technology meant we went paperless, everyone had to fill out a blue form with their personal information for customs.

NBA players get a lot of preferential treatment, but to enter the country, they couldn't avoid this. Except, they didn't even have to fill out the forms. The team would do it for them. When we landed at Pearson airport, the plane would be taxied to the North Lounge on Derry, a customs officer would come on the plane and stand at the front, and you could give him the blue form and you went on your way.

That was it. Maybe post-9/11 it's changed a bit, but certainly not much. The NBA ran charter flights for its staff and media who wanted to pay for a seat during the 2019 NBA finals out of Toronto, and trust me, as a guy who flies commercial and has for 25 years, it's a relative piece of cake. Dedicated airline employees to walk you through baggage drop, dedicated airport personnel to walk you through security checks, more airline personnel to walk you through a dedicated U.S. customs line that's as easy as Nexus or Global Entry. Trying, distracting, difficult it is not.

This was the thing stopping players from wanting to play in Canada? Craziness.

It's always been insulting to hear about these complaints. People made it sound like you were moving to a third-world country when you signed with the Raptors. These players thought they were travelling to a whole different world. All you did was whatever a regular citizen had to do when they crossed the border.

I don't want to generalize to all American players, but a lot of them grow up not thinking playing in the NBA would mean moving to another country, so I think there's a lot of bias and stereotypes that they simply believe. Anything that isn't the process they were used to growing up is a nuisance. A lot of these guys were just petulant little kids.

The international players never really minded. Back then, Žan Tabak, who was part of the expansion team, was on a Croatian passport. There were other issues he had to deal with when he crossed borders, but he didn't care, he didn't make a fuss. He had a work visa to play for the Raptors. It was just what you did when you travelled. Rarely did I ever hear any European players complain about this. The team did all it could to expedite or ease the process, too. They had liaisons with the federal government who helped procure work visas; they did most if not all of the paperwork for players wanting to bring their families to Toronto.

It's bias born out of ignorance. I sometimes think about how these players who come to Toronto to play don't appreciate all the good that comes from getting out of their United States. The foreign exchange rate is different now. Back then, when you played here, your contract was paid in American dollars, but you spent everything here—expenses, housing, food, entertainment—in Canadian dollars. It was like getting a 33 percent raise.

And speaking of entertainment, let me tell you, for a lot of NBA players, especially the younger guys who liked to go out and have fun, Toronto offered them a kind of anonymity that they wouldn't get in New York or Los Angeles. And this was way before social media where you can't go anywhere without one or 20 videos coming out showing exactly what you were up to after the game. Certain players definitely enjoyed the limelight and frequented different strip clubs in the city.

There was one strip club called Fantasia that became an unofficial social club for the Raptors. It became this running joke. It was located up in Thornhill and off the beaten path. Few people even knew that NBA players had turned this into their go-to hangout. You didn't hear a peep about it. They could live the life they wanted.

Have you ever heard about Bernie Offstein, a long-time basketball face in Toronto who was the team's first security director? His day job was in criminal intelligence and as a police liaison with Revenue Canada. He was the go-to guy to make things go away, a fixer, if you will. If there was a big drug bust at the airport, Bernie was the guy. He knew everyone and everything. Oliver Miller, and others, were gun owners. It was entirely legal where they had lived and entirely illegal where they worked, and sometimes they just didn't understand that fact. They had weapons and they brought them, or tried to bring them, to their new homes. Bernie would get wind of it, and the message was clear: "You can't have guns here in Canada." He made the whole thing go away. You never heard a peep about these guys.

Of course, you had to actually play here to appreciate the benefits, and getting players to even commit to that was impossible.

If it wasn't the whole customs thing, it was that players didn't know about the tax system here and just assumed that being here meant they would be placed in a perilous position financially. Glen Grunwald, when he was the assistant general manager, hired an accounting firm to come up with a tax plan for the team. Players learned things like why it was better off for them to buy instead of rent. They had to have the days of residency issues explained. Grunwald educated the players and also their agents. It was a whole league-wide thing.

The team didn't love having to do this, but they had no choice. If agents couldn't communicate the proper set of facts to their clients, no player would ever come to Toronto. They had to let the players know that if you come to Toronto, it doesn't mean you suddenly lose millions of dollars out of your pocket. Grunwald went to great lengths to do that. He spent a lot of time on this particular side of things, so credit to him for changing the conversation a little.

There were plenty of players who came here and saw Toronto for what it was: a beautiful metropolitan city with great restaurants and a wonderful nightlife, and not a bad place at all to raise a family. Guys like DeMar DeRozan and Kyle Lowry—they could have gone anywhere during their free agency, but they had experienced Toronto and loved it enough to stay. (Winning and being paid millions of dollars helps, too, but that's the same for every NBA team.)

And yet, even as Grunwald and the organization tried their best, guys would play in Toronto and find new things to complain about. Everyone complained that they couldn't watch ESPN here. Chris Bosh got here as a rookie and would tell me that he couldn't watch SportsCenter. But the team would always accommodate. I'm not sure how legal they were, but there were always ways to watch the television channels you wanted.

When Antonio Davis was negotiating his new contract with the

Raptors, he complained about the metric system here in Canada, compared to the United States. Valid concerns, perhaps, but also a pretty smart negotiating ploy. Glen Grunwald, an American-born executive who assimilated quite well in a new environment, offered jokingly to tutor the kids, but it was a perfect example of how the smallest of changes to lifestyle could be turned into concerns. It wasn't that Canada was bad, per se; it was that it was different and different can be scary. That Toronto and Canada were more worldly than the insular United States was almost too much for some players to bear. I always thought they were the losers in the bigger picture, an opinion shared by many.

What else? The bags of milk. That was new. The weather too, of course. Whenever I hear people complain about the cold, I laugh, if only because it's not like we're some vast wasteland of snow, cold, and wind. These were guys who had played or maybe lived in cities like Chicago or Minneapolis or Boston or Milwaukee or Detroit. Those were not subtropical climes and not at all different from Toronto where weather is concerned. It's almost as though people just want to come up with excuses about Toronto, like a winter storm only hits north of the border.

Remember Kawhi Leonard famously saying he could go from door to door for the game? His facetiousness aside, Leonard had a point. These players lived in condos with underground parking and drove (or were driven) to the underground parking lot at the arena. They never had to be outside.

Some of the players who would come here resented the perception, too, that they had been sent to a wasteland. Especially in those early years when the team wasn't winning at all, it was like you weren't actually part of the NBA when you played for the Raptors.

So some of them were resentful. It was like the league saw them as second-class citizens. Others felt motivated by it. It gave them a reason to fight harder or give up.

I personally think it's a really good life experience for these guys. Some of the vets especially came to appreciate how cool it was to live in another country, I think. Even the head coaches, too, came to appreciate it.

Dwane Casey is a really good example. Toronto was a completely different environment for his kids. DeRozan and Lowry said the same things to me, too, that they were glad their kids got to spend some of their formative years here in Toronto (and in Lowry's case, continue to spend).

The one guy who I will credit for changing the perception is Vince Carter. When he came here, you didn't hear him complain; he would keep talking up Toronto in his interviews. And that was important. He held a charity game for a couple of summers in an effort to show his fellow NBAers that the city had plenty to offer. Kenny Anderson didn't want to come. Tracy McGrady had left in free agency. And here came this phenom who graced magazine covers and captured the world with his Slam Dunk Contest, all the while wearing a Toronto Raptors jersey. He truly liked the city and appreciated the lifestyle, its cosmopolitan nature, its diversity. And he told anyone who asked that it was not at all a bad place to play.

I always thought that much of the Trouble with Toronto, if you will, came from the fact that the Raptors weren't a very good team for an awful lot of years. Combining a team that didn't win with a city that few knew fed into this anti-Toronto attitude out there, but I figured that once the Raptors were successful, most of it would go away.

And that's what happened. For a city that was so bad, it was telling that just about every single significant player who could re-sign here did—Vince Carter, Chris Bosh, Charles Oakley, Antonio Davis, Kyle Lowry, DeMar DeRozan. They all could have left and didn't when they first had the chance; it had to say something about the team and the city that ran counter to some odd public perceptions.

The fact is, Toronto is now a desired destination for some players. They love the city for the charms it offers away from the game, the restaurants and clubs and lifestyle. They like the Raptors because the team wins and it pays its players and it's a first-rate organization.

All the anti-Toronto palaver of the first few years of the franchise is gone; the metric system still exists, taxes are still complicated, it gets cold at times, and nope, there's still no ESPN on the television dial, but somehow, Toronto is good.

As it always was.

4

ISIAH THOMAS

He was the first president, the first big-name hire, the first guy asked to build something out of nothing. As an expansion franchise, the Toronto Raptors needed a starting point. Yes, they had an arena, a nickname, they had players, a head coach, and everything needed to call themselves an NBA organization. But someone had to steer the ship. And the person who did all the heavy lifting in those early years was Isiah Thomas.

Thomas arrived in Toronto with a stellar résumé as a player. A two-time NBA champion, NBA finals MVP, and a 12-time all-star who was the leader of the "Bad Boy" Detroit Pistons, Thomas was one of the best point guards to have ever played the game. Now, he was running point on something else: making people care about basketball in Toronto.

Today, Scotiabank Arena is packed with fans on a nightly basis. And when the playoffs arrive—and the Raptors have become a post-season mainstay—fans not only pack Jurassic Park outside of the arena but also gather in viewing parties across the country. Back when the Raptors joined the NBA in 1995, this wasn't the case. Thomas had to navigate a city that was obsessed with hockey, and not exactly a basketball hotbed.

For the longest time, you could buy tickets at Pizza Pizza or at Shoppers Drug Mart and if you wanted Maple Leafs tickets, you had to buy Raptors tickets. It was cross-marketing but it was important. There was a series of television commercials starring Raptors as Leafs fans. Doug Christie told me in 2019 that he still has a Mats Sundin jersey he used as a prop in his TV bit. Thomas may not have liked it that much—the Raptors very much wanted to stand as their own entity and not get too dependent on the hockey crowd—but you did what you had to do back in those early days.

Thomas was aware of all the challenges. He would often pick the brains of the writers, too. We would chat on a regular basis. He would ask me, "What are the people saying? How do we sell tickets?" He wanted to know what was happening in the city, and he valued opinions of people like me, who knew Toronto and the sporting landscape I spent years in better than he did.

Thomas was also a friend and a confidant. We would chat about life. We always talked about having a burger at his favourite place in Detroit; regrettably, we never did. We used to talk all the time; I remember Isiah would call every day. After my son was born in August of 1996, he called and said, "Look, I know your life has changed, but can we still talk every day?" Sure, maybe we were being used a little bit, but having constant access to the man in charge was never a bad thing. It was a symbiotic relationship—he needed us as much as we needed him—but it worked and fostered good relations that all of us appreciated.

I remember when I went to Detroit to cover his jersey retirement ceremony and people were grilling him about taking the job in

Toronto. Everyone had presumed he would be a Piston for life, a fact openly stated at one time by Detroit owner Bill Davidson. I remember that when Thomas walked out of the press conference, he grabbed me and Craig Daniels of the *Toronto Sun* and said, "If you ever turn into those motherfuckers like that, we will never speak again."

Thomas was decisive. Even with an expansion team, he had a competitive spirit, he wanted to win. One of the first draft picks he made was Jimmy King, from the famous Fab Five Michigan Wolverines. King wasn't the hardest-working guy, and in the first season, there was a period when he was out with a muscle problem. It could have been real, but Thomas had to make sure. There was one time in practice Thomas grabbed King by the thigh and just gave it a squeeze. He was sending a message, letting the team know there was no lollygagging allowed.

There was also a charm about him. It worked well, especially in the early years. I remember telling Thomas that basketball would sell on its own and he didn't need to constantly compare it to hockey. The best thing to do was to find new fans, and he should know that you weren't going to convert people who were lifelong Toronto Maple Leafs fans. There were enough people in the city who wanted something new.

Thomas would talk to anyone in the community. He would talk to other media members. He would talk to service clubs. And he knew about deadlines. If you called his assistant at ten in the morning, she would ask about your newspaper deadline and when you would need him by, and she would make sure Thomas spoke to you before that.

Thomas was very hands-on. He brought in people that he knew. The first head coach, Brendan Malone, was a former assistant coach with the Detroit Pistons. Players like John Salley and Earl Cureton had a history with Thomas as well. He was building an organization that was very much his own.

Thomas had an unbelievable eye for talent as well, especially with the draft. Look at his track record while he was here. His three first-round picks were Damon Stoudamire, Marcus Camby, and Tracy McGrady. Stoudamire turned out just fine, but in that first draft, Thomas made it known he wanted a high school player named Kevin Garnett. The plan was to let Garnett play only home games in Toronto because he was a high school kid. He ended up going to the Minnesota Timberwolves with the number-five pick in the draft.

Thomas was a really ambitious person, which made him the right person for the job. He wasn't just trying to make basketball a thing in Toronto, he wanted to be an innovator. Thomas told me one time that he wanted to change how pre-game layup lines ran. He wanted to change the old structure and have guys actually practice something useful, like running offensive sets before tipoff. He was a positionless basketball kind of guy before it became en vogue. It didn't happen, but it at least showed that the Raptors had some kind of forward thinking coming from the very top of the organization.

The ambition is perhaps why Thomas's tenure was cut short in the Raptors' third season. It was a crisis year in which the team would lose the two faces of their franchise: Stoudamire and Thomas. In November, co-owner Allan Slaight invoked what is known as a "shotgun" clause, which forced the team's other owner, John Bitove, to come up with about $65 million to purchase Slaight's 39.5 percent stake or sell. Bitove, who had brought Thomas into the fold and was completely aligned with him, was unable to come up with the money and Slaight became the primary owner. Thomas and Bitove had worked until the last possible minute to gain control, but when the plan fell through, Bitove left and Slaight became the owner of the team overnight. From that point on, the writing was on the wall; it was clear Thomas would be moving on at some point.

Slaight was a straight businessman. He was nice, philanthropic, but he wasn't the dynamic personality that either of the other men were. Bitove and Thomas were the dynamic team. They were personable. They were public—in many ways, Thomas *was* the Raptors. And his departure was not unexpected. He and Slaight were not close, they were dissimilar personalities and at different stages of their lives, and it was just a matter of time before the split came. At one point, after Thomas had left and I had written something complimentary about him, I got a call from Slaight. He disputed much of what I'd written and offered me access to private files in a private boardroom of his downtown office complex under the provision that I not copy or take any of the correspondence. It was complex business and financial stuff, nothing I had any acumen in, and I remember leaving with the thought that Thomas had grand plans—what ultimately became Maple Leaf Sports & Entertainment (MLSE)—and just lacked the money and support to put them together. Whether that was his fault or someone else's fault or simply one of those things that happen in the world of high finance, big business, and big ego, I don't know. I do know that Thomas anticipated things as they eventually turned out with the creation of MLSE, a conglomerate that includes several different sports properties, but that he never got a chance to see it through.

I was home one morning when I got a call from Bitove telling me Thomas was leaving and that an announcement was coming in the afternoon. I called my colleague Chris Young to fill him in and ask for his guidance and help. We didn't know what was going on and decided to make a few calls. It was confirmed that Thomas was leaving and was going to be a television analyst at NBC. We were all aware there were some issues with ownership and that perhaps he was looking to get out.

I had a meeting with our managing editor in the afternoon and told him we needed to put the story on the front page of the *Toronto Star*. He wasn't convinced. He said that people wouldn't really care. I had to tell him, This is the face of the franchise leaving. This is a huge deal. He told me to write the story and show him. I wrote it. I showed him. And it was on the front page. They had no idea how it would resonate with the fan base. After the article came out, I remember the managing editor telling me, It's pretty big. People are talking about it.

After the dust settled, a few days later, I had a chance to talk to Thomas. I remember him telling me, Sorry it didn't work out, but it was time to go. This wasn't what he signed up for. You have to remember, the third year was a complete crisis point for the franchise. The Raptors had yet to fall under the MLSE umbrella. And there were legitimate questions by then of whether the franchise was viable long-term in Toronto.

I talked to commissioner David Stern two years after Thomas's departure. And he told me that every business goes through major changes early on, but when you're an NBA franchise, it just happens to play out more publicly than, say, a company operating in another industry. The league wasn't concerned about the Raptors because what happened was not unusual in the world of business. And he turned out to be right. But that was a difficult year. I remember Glen Grunwald walking out to address the crowd at the end of a 16–66 season in front of the home crowd at Maple Leaf Gardens. They booed him. They booed him long and loud. I believed basketball was going to work. But at that very moment, I did think that maybe this thing wasn't going to last for long.

I know things with Thomas don't always end well, and he has his fair share of enemies and detractors in the game to this day. He failed to turn the Continental Basketball Association into a solid minor league feeding system or even a solid business. He will forever be scarred by his time with the New York Knicks, which included a sexual harassment and employment lawsuit filed against him and the team owner while he was the president. It was eventually settled for about $12 million.

And that is absolutely part of his legacy. But before all of that, while he was the president of the organization I was so closely linked to—one that became central to the sporting fabric of the entire country after he got it started on the path—he was nothing but helpful and good at his job.

And caring.

You may remember an early Raptor named Carlos Rogers, a somewhat promising young player Thomas traded for before the first season got underway.

Rogers's sister, Rene, developed serious complications in 1997 from a kidney transplant she had received in 1992, and Carlos was ready to donate one of his own—he was compatible and it would have cost him his career, but he didn't care.

Thomas was incredibly supportive every step of the way, and his compassion reached its zenith the day Rene eventually died before a transplant could be performed. The family wanted the Raptors, who were playing that night, to hold off telling Carlos that his sister was in critical condition; Thomas was having none of that.

"He threw the phone down, grabbed me, and ran—literally ran—down the street to get Carlos," Rick Kaplan, then a member of

Toronto's media relations staff, told reporters. "Carlos only lives about a quarter of a mile away, so Isiah ran. You won't see many general managers do that."

No, you won't. And that's the side of Thomas I'll appreciate.

How would the Raptors franchise have been different if Thomas had stayed? It's hard to say. I don't know if the team would have ended up with MLSE. Back then, the goal was to build an arena for each team. The Raptors wanted to build their own arena. At one point, it was going to be above Union Station. Or on Bay Street. But it never went beyond just a pipe dream. It wouldn't have made sense to have two buildings, though. The only thing that made sense was for the Raptors and the Leafs to get together financially. Who knows, though? Thomas always thought he could turn the franchise into something on its own—something that would be huge, even bigger than hockey. I think he thought eventually the Raptors would reach a point where he could buy the Leafs. He was that ambitious.

The Raptors wouldn't be possible now without what Isiah Thomas did in those early years. But like everything else with the franchise in those first few years, whenever something good happened, something would come along and sweep it away. The team had its first face of the franchise, and he was gone before the end of their third season.

5

FIRST COACHES

It's been fascinating over the first 25 years of covering the Raptors to watch how the playing roster has evolved and to see the difficult, elusive search for the right mix of personalities and abilities that will lead to sustained success and championship contention year after year after year.

It's truly been an ongoing experiment; sometimes it works and things click, but more often than not, over the first 15 or 17 or 19 seasons, it fell short, for one reason or another.

Maybe talents didn't mix—too many so-so shooters, too much inexperience, just not enough skill.

Maybe personalities didn't mesh—hindering the necessary desire to play for the guy sitting next to you instead of for yourself. Team-building can be an imprecise exercise.

But it has been equally fascinating watching the franchise go from coach to coach to coach to coach, nine overall in the first 25 years of the Raptors' existence, always searching for the right voice, the right philosophy, the right ability to draw the best out of whatever players were available. Often it failed, and they lurched from one to the other to the next, until the last seven seasons, when they found stability and success first with Dwane Casey and then Nick Nurse, who were finally able to coax the maximum out of each of their teams to get them to win and contend and grow.

And, man, did they run the gamut of coaches, trying to figure out who best fit.

Some were sacrificial lambs who were caretakers rather than long-term solutions, some were hired primarily because they were diametrically different from the guy who went before them, and many were inherited by new general managers who had bigger issues to deal with than immediately bringing in "their" guy. And it's been a roller coaster of personalities—and stories—over the years.

Brendan Malone was the first and, like so many things around that first franchise, we didn't know much about him. And he certainly didn't know much about us. As things tended to work back then, he got hired primarily because of familiarity with Isiah Thomas. He'd been an assistant to Chuck Daly with those wonderful Detroit Pistons' championship "Bad Boy" teams that Thomas led, and having a coach who'd do the general manager's bidding was the right way to go, everyone thought.

Except it wasn't.

Malone wanted to win; it was part of his DNA, and if he had precious little experienced talent to work with, he was going to milk it for all it was worth, player development be damned. And it didn't take too long for him to butt heads with his boss. One of the worst losses in the franchise was a 126–86 hammering administered by the Orlando Magic in March of 1996, and by that time in the season, the Raptors—and Thomas—were demanding that Malone play kids to see what they had rather than vets who would give them a better chance to win every game.

Well, Malone basically played nothing but overmatched guards for the entire night against the likes of Shaquille O'Neal and Penny Hardaway, with predictable results.

At halftime, a seething Thomas held an impromptu scrum in the SkyDome work area—"This is not what I had in mind," he basically spat out—and I think we all knew Malone's days were numbered right then.

But Malone, in many ways, was great for us. He was patient with media members who didn't understand the intricacies of the game, and since he was New York born and bred, he was a rabid New York Rangers fan who loved to remind us that the Leafs had been losers for years.

The end of his one-year tenure came expectedly on the last day of the regular season, following an eminently forgettable game against the Philadelphia 76ers, and he knew it was coming. A dear friend—long-time now deceased Philly writer Phil Jasner—and I were hanging about before the game and Phil said, "Let's go talk to Brendan," who was an old friend of his. We walked into the locker room while Brendan was diagramming plays on the whiteboard—last game of a lost season and the guy was still working—and Phil said, "Don't worry, Brendan, do your work and we'll catch up after the game."

"No, Phil," Brendan said. "I'm getting fired after the game, let's talk now."

Sure enough when Brendan got back to the hotel room that night, which had served as his home for the entire season, he found his separation papers had been slid under the door; he was gone after one season.

But like so much of that first incarnation of the team, Malone's departure just portended things to come and, boy oh boy, his immediate successor, Darrell Walker, went out with an even bigger bang.

Walker was another good guy in a no-win situation. He'd been an assistant to Malone and was another friend of Isiah who might have been a bit overmatched as a first-time NBA head coach. He was a good storyteller and a hail-fellow-well-met kind of guy, but I always thought he liked the idea of being an NBA head coach more than he liked having to do the work to be a successful one.

Of course, he was saddled with a mediocre team at best—that he coaxed it to 30 wins in the second season was impressive given the talent at his disposal—and his tenure was short but not entirely sweet. After his benefactor, Thomas, left on the eve of the third season, we all wondered how long he would last. And when the Raptors lost the first two games of the season, won their third, and then lost a franchise record 17 straight games, I knew he'd never survive.

It's not that he wasn't good, it's that he barely cared once the season was in the toilet, and if things were going to get turned around, everyone in a position of leadership had to be resolute in doing their part.

Darrell? In one of his very first meetings with new general manager Glen Grunwald, he wanted to make sure he'd get paid in full when he was fired rather than join his bosses in trying to turn things around. It didn't make Walker a bad guy—it made him a realist more worried about himself than the team. I didn't think that would ever fly.

It didn't.

When he was fired, I was actually in Nagano covering the 1998 Winter Olympics, but the scene on his last day has gone down in franchise lore. The Raptors were in New Jersey, staying at the Sheraton Meadowlands right across from the arena, a kind of dumpy old hotel that teams used for its proximity to the arena rather than its opulence. It had an open-concept lobby, and after he got a fax of his separation papers, Walker strode through the lobby singing, "Free at last, free at last. Thank God almighty, I'm free at last."

It was not a shining moment, but it was in keeping with the narrative over the first few years—that the Raptors were a better story than a team—which continued unabated with the coaches for another decade or so.

I'm often asked who I think the "best" coach in Raptors history has been, and in many ways, it's an impossible question to answer. How one guy coaches the team he's got to deal with is impossible to compare to how someone else would do with some entirely different group of players or circumstances to handle. But there's no denying, I don't think, that Butch Carter, who followed Walker in the job, was among the most creative.

Carter was a really good in-game coach. I remember a game in Detroit when he put in two of his own guys to guard the inbounder during an end-of-game possession. I had never seen a coach do that before. It helped them win the game.

Carter had a lot of moving parts. It always felt like he had something else going on concurrently with coaching the team. The night before the Raptors were prepared to play in their first-ever playoff series against New York, me and a bunch of reporters were having dinner with Grunwald when news broke. Carter was suing Marcus Camby, a member of the Knicks. It was a $5 million defamation suit because Camby had called Carter a liar in an interview.

I asked Grunwald if he was aware of this. "Oh my god," he said. "I thought we had talked him out of that."

The last straw came when Carter tried to go above Grunwald and get himself promoted to general manager. (In this hypothetical scenario, Grunwald would have moved into a president position.) That was the thing with Carter: he was always trying to manoeuvre his way into something bigger.

Carter's thinking was that this promotion would put him closer to agents and players in the game. It was a power grab. And that turned out to be the last straw for the organization. Carter was fired even after leading the Raptors to their first playoff berth.

The Raptors needed someone who would be the antithesis of Carter. They needed someone calm, someone who wasn't going to create headlines. In came Lenny Wilkens, one of the most successful and longest-tenured NBA head coaches in league history.

"There was no second choice," Grunwald said at the time.

I always used to say Lenny was retired when he took the Raptors job, he just didn't tell anybody. It was well known that he wasn't exactly the hardest-working guy in the business.

In his last season here, the Raptors went into Washington with like eight guys and multiple players on 10-day contracts, and upset Michael Jordan and the Wizards. It was a huge upset, a big win that had everyone pumped. The team got on the plane and was going home, excited and energized. One of the team staffers mentioned that they had to get ready for tomorrow's game.

Wilkens replied, "Who do we play tomorrow?"

Wilkens's greatest accomplishment here was turning Alvin Williams into a starting point guard. For some reason, Carter never liked Williams. He buried him at the end of the bench. When Wilkens came, they connected as point guards.

Wilkens trusted Williams. He let him play, gave him way more responsibility, and it instilled a lot of confidence in the young guy.

To this day, Williams swears by Wilkens and gives him full credit for jump-starting his NBA career.

After Wilkens, things got even weirder. The Raptors hired Kevin O'Neill. We still have no idea why he was the choice, but the story goes O'Neill was highly recommended by a bunch of guys around the league.

O'Neill was a hard-working guy but also very controlling. He made every play call, and because of his old-school approach, he wanted to win games with scores in the 70s and 80s. He went against the direction of the modern game and wanted his team to grind out victories. You could see it in his personality. He was a "crash and burn" guy right from the start.

He lasted only one season in Toronto. The team went 33–49, but he left behind some memorable moments. One night in San Francisco, the Raptors had won in overtime against Golden State and pushed their record to 25–25. It appeared they had a chance to make the playoffs, but Jalen Rose broke his hand that night and all hope went out the window. Frustrated, O'Neill broke a lamp in his hotel room.

A month later, *The Globe and Mail* broke the story, in a piece that also talked about his lifestyle and how he loved having a few drinks too many on a lot of nights. We woke up the next day to go to a shootaround in New York, and you can imagine the number of media members circling the scene at Madison Square Garden. To his credit, O'Neill answered every question and took all responsibility. He looked at a group of reporters, including me at one point, and said, "Look, I've only been drunk on the road one time this season and that was with you, Doug." He was referring to the night before a game in Seattle when we hung out and had a few too many drinks at the Metropolitan. I felt like three inches tall when he said that, but he was right. There were a lot of beers involved that evening.

O'Neill was a train wreck waiting to happen. After the Raptors played their final game of the season in Milwaukee, we were all scheduled to fly home. O'Neill asked me what time my flight was. I told him I would land around eleven in the morning back in Toronto. "You're going to want to move that up," he said. "My press conference is something you want to be at."

He wasn't wrong. At his end-of-season presser, O'Neill blasted the organization and questioned their commitment to winning. Later that day, he was fired. And you want to know how crazy O'Neill could be? That night, long after we'd all filed our stories, we were in the old Harbour Sports Grille, a drinking establishment right by the arena that was the local for all the beat writers. We were in the bar and assistant Jay Triano—who O'Neill always thought was some kind of front-office plant even though that was the furthest thing from the truth—was in the dining room with his family, wife and three kids. Then O'Neill, along with a couple of his other staff members who'd obviously been out for a few to mark the end of his tenure, tried to get into the place to get at Triano, and only the forceful words of the joint's owner stopped a really ugly incident from happening.

The coaching carousel continued, and in came Sam Mitchell, who, surprise, was the exact opposite of the previous coach. Unlike O'Neill, Mitchell was personable and would spend hours chatting with us, not just about the game of basketball, but about politics, the economy, and anything else that came up. He loved to talk and he loved to tell stories.

Mitchell was a worldly guy. We were in Oklahoma City one time when he grabbed a bunch of reporters and got us all to go with him to visit the Oklahoma City National Memorial & Museum. I remember seeing Sam almost in tears just talking about the tragedy of the 1995 Oklahoma City bombing, and how that wasn't the America he loved. It was a very poignant moment that gave us a glimpse into the person Mitchell was.

I think Bryan Colangelo fired Mitchell too quickly. The team was coming off back-to-back playoff appearances but started the 2010–11 season 8–9. After a blowout loss in Denver, Mitchell was let go. I've always felt it was an overreaction to a poor start. I would have liked to see Mitchell coach a little bit more of that team. He wasn't a bad coach at all. But the organization felt like they needed a new voice.

Mitchell's replacement was Jay Triano, who many saw as a token Canadian hire. Triano had been around the game a long time, and I think Colangelo wanted someone who would listen to his input without much pushback. Mitchell had done it reluctantly.

It was a no-win situation for Triano. He inherited the team at a time when the roster was going in the wrong direction. It wasn't until the Raptors hired Dwane Casey in 2011 that the team finally found stability at the head coaching position.

Even though they all had their flaws, I'll never forget the head coaches who came before that.

It's funny how relationships develop. As a guy who came to the beat with a few years in the business—I was 35 when the inaugural season rolled around—it was easier to develop relationships with coaches who were of the same vintage or close to it than with players who were much younger and focused on different things.

Maybe because of that, I tended to give coaches a break. One of the true tenets of writing about any team is that a coach often gets too much blame when things go south and too much credit when things are good. If there is one thing I learned early, it's that the NBA is a players league and that talent wins; the X and O skills of any one coach can only do so much.

6

THE FANS

It's impossible to write a book about the Toronto Raptors without talking about their fans: fans who've been through all the ups and downs—mostly a lot of low points for the first two decades with occasional blips of competence—but who always showed up, always cheered, and who were finally rewarded with a championship that they will savour forever.

And to think that this fan base came from such humble beginnings. If I'm being honest, a large number of Raptors fans who showed up to the SkyDome and watched the expansion team on their television sets were not very familiar with NBA basketball. There was certainly a subset of hardcore basketball fans who knew the ins and outs, the X's and O's, but there were also a lot of people who had no idea what was going on. Maybe you couldn't really blame them. I mean, the 500-level seats at the SkyDome were atrocious. My wife and I had season tickets in the second row of the 500 level. You would basically be watching the scoreboard.

For the fans, one of the constants from day one has been The

Raptor, the mascot who has been played by the same guy since the very start. I'm not a huge fan of the extraneous stuff that goes on around an NBA game, but I most certainly have an affinity for The Raptor, and at times in the first few seasons, it was about the most entertaining thing at the gym some nights.

Two quick stories about The Raptor.

He's so committed to his job, and the character, that he actually proposed to his wife while in costume on the day of the first Naismith Cup game between the Raptors and Vancouver Grizzlies in Winnipeg. He had strong connections to that city, still does, and it strikes me as a perfect way to start a relationship, one that thrives to this day.

A lot of us, of course, know who is under the costume and count him among our friends. In the hours before any home game, we'll be sitting on the seats along the baseline catching up, and he's invariably there. I've had guests who'd sit there with me on occasion watching the players warm up and, invariably, the out-of-costume Raptor will stop by. We'll chat, I'll introduce him to my guests, and when the game's over and I'm checking to see if they've had a good time, I'll ask them how they liked The Raptor. They are always full of praise and then stunned when I tell them they met him before the game. Gives me some cachet with them that I know such famous stuffed animals so well.

The one consistent thing about this fan base is that they've always showed up. The expansion years. The Vince Carter era. All the years after the Vince Carter era when the franchise repeatedly fumbled at building something competent and sustainable. The brief hope that Chris Bosh brought, which was extinguished when he went to Miami. And all those lean years before Masai Ujiri, Dwane Casey, DeMar DeRozan, and Kyle Lowry ushered in the We the North era.

The one constant fan from day one was Nav Bhatia. The superfan, as he would come to be known, was there from the beginning and became the most recognizable figure in the Raptors fan base. Nav was more than just a fan. The first time I got to know him was when Vince was here and Nav became close friends with his mom, Michelle.

Nav was very humble; he hadn't become the star that he is today. He was a local car salesman, and he wanted to help his Sikh community get into as many games as possible. He was buying tickets in the stands for kids to come watch the Raptors. Every year, he'd host a Baisakhi Day celebration—a Sikh religious holiday—and he would be steadfast in his desire to make sure everyone joined in the celebration or at least knew what it was for. He was omnipresent. He would always be there when you least expected him. We would bump into him on road trips and be like, here's this fucking guy again.

Because of his courtside seats on the baseline, opposing players got to know him as well. He would wave a towel proudly when opposing teams shot free throws or to celebrate a Raptors basket. That's when Nav started becoming recognizable. He brought a lot of people from his community into basketball. He helped the franchise reach a group of people they wouldn't have been able to on their own, at least not to the extent that Nav was able to with his influence and reach.

I give him a lot of credit. He spent a lot of money out of his own pocket to be there and to support the Raptors. He travelled on his own dime. I don't think he was given a lot of free tickets. He also got to know the players, and he'd help them whether it was with cars, housing, or being introduced to people around the city. There was a symbiotic relationship between Nav and the guys on the team.

Nav was also smart and recognized his influence. He was a huge defender of Michelle, who wasn't particularly well liked by certain parts of the fan base while Vince Carter was here. There was a whole controversy about how Michelle had her own parking spot and how the franchise catered to Vince. Michelle even criticized the Raptors and some of Vince's teammates, and Vince got the reputation that he was a momma's boy. Nav helped to defuse the tension between Michelle and the fan base. It wasn't that Nav got Michelle any kind of legitimacy by being friends with her, but he was very inclusive. I remember a few years ago, Michelle showed up to a Raptors game sitting next to Nav. They remain very good friends to this day.

Whether the Raptors were winning or not, Nav was always there, and that counts for something. Some people were upset when he received a championship ring on behalf of the organization in 2019, but he is part of the Raptors family. I can't imagine how much money he's spent of his own throughout the 25 years of supporting this team. In terms of superfans around the league, Nav is one of a kind. A little less demonstrative than Spike Lee, but more in your face than Jack Nicholson.

The thing for me is that Nav couldn't have existed as, say, a Maple Leafs superfan. First, hockey just isn't as interactive. He wouldn't have been able to be part of the in-game experience sitting courtside. And also, he reflected the demographic of the Raptors fan base, which certainly is a lot more diverse and less homogeneous than that of the Leafs.

For a very long time, people within NBA circles would talk about the fan base in Toronto and how great it was. Towards the end of Vince's time here, Rick Carlisle came into town to play the Raptors, and I remember he stood on the court, pointed up to where the people sat in the upper levels, and told me, "I can't believe this is the best kept secret in the NBA. The fans here, it's always loud, and they're always here."

The interaction stuck with me. This wasn't just some rookie visiting head coach, blowing smoke to local media members here in Toronto. Carlisle wasn't that kind of guy. He had played with the Celtics in the vaunted and legendary Boston Garden. He had coached with the Pacers, and Indiana is known for their home court advantage as well. He had seen it all, and the respect he was paying the Raptors fans was real.

Of course, this would remain a well-guarded secret mostly thanks to the Raptors being a very incompetent franchise for a long time. When you don't win, it's hard to showcase the fans that you have. This would change once MLSE president Tim Leiweke and team president Masai Ujiri arrived. Off the court, their biggest splash at the time, before the Raptors got good again, was introducing Drake as their global ambassador. He would, like Nav, become synonymous with the Raptors brand.

I had no idea who Drake was. But I knew he resonated with a lot of kids, and that was the most important part. The players knew who he was. He was the first guy with cultural influence outside the game of basketball to embrace the Raptors brand in this way. It was an over-the-top Tim Leiweke move. He thought it would be bombastic. Suddenly, people who weren't Raptors fans heard of the connection with Drake and decided to watch the game. At first I was like, What the fuck is Leiweke doing? Well, it turned out pretty good.

And give Leiweke credit for tapping into something that is uniquely Toronto.

"There's nothing to dislike about Drake," Leiweke once said. "I think it's amazing the time and the emotion and the passion he's put into not just the organization but the city. I understand that there are those that find his emotions to be unchecked. I see it the other way, which is if you look at We the North, that was inspired by Drake."

I still remember the first time they had a Drake Night at the arena. They brought Drake into the press conference room where the head coach usually does his pre-game chat and I asked him, "Generally, people have to be dead before they get a *night*. Why do you get a night?" He took the question in and laughed and said, "I appreciate all of this."

I give him all the credit in the world. He is a legitimate fan of the Raptors and was even long before he became one of the most famous people on earth. He's not getting paid, and what would he really gain from this even if he was? Does it mean anything to him to add another million to his portfolio? He's doing this because he actually cares about the Raptors.

I never thought Drake would be able to do much in terms of recruiting players, but at the same time, it can't hurt. You get a guy like this associated with the team, it helps the brand. And I appreciate how much fun Drake has at games. He doesn't just sit there passively and watch. He's cheering, massaging Nick's shoulders, taunting opposing players. People take issue with it because he's famous, but he's not really doing anything different from a guy sitting three rows down from him. I don't think he's distracting the players or the game. It just speaks to the passion of the sport. I've got no problem with Drake being who he is.

The turning point for this fan base and the franchise was 2014. They were supposed to go in the tank, but suddenly, after trading Rudy Gay to Sacramento, the team took off behind Kyle and DeMar and had home court advantage in the first round against the Brooklyn Nets. It was unbelievable to see what we have now come to expect from every single Raptors playoff game: thousands of fans gathered outside Scotiabank Arena in Maple Leaf Square, the space now nicknamed Jurassic Park.

People just wanted to be part of the experience. It became a thing synonymous with the Toronto Raptors. When Masai Ujiri went outside and addressed the fans and said "Fuck Brooklyn," I was in the arena, getting ready for tipoff, and we just couldn't believe it. It became a rallying cry. It certainly created a buzz. Give Masai credit too for connecting and rallying the fans. He's personable and speaks a language that they understand. It's always a *we* thing with Masai. He makes the fans feel like they're part of the experience.

The bus rides to Detroit, and Masai being a part of them, are such a great thing for the fans. You wouldn't see Pat Gillick or Ken Dryden sitting on a bus with fans for four and a half hours. The fans appreciate that connection. The way he engages the fan base is I think part of the reason why they are so supportive of the Raptors. They see a guy they really like and they see a guy who they think they know.

The Raptors lost that series on a Game 7 at home. I will never forget the home crowd that day. It was a Sunday afternoon game, and because it had become a national broadcast, three seats opened up on the floor level, and PR guru Jim LaBumbard moved me, Ryan Wolstat, and Michael Grange courtside. We hadn't been courtside in years. To this day, even with the Raptors having won a championship, I still haven't heard the crowd as loud as on that day. They didn't shut up and were on their feet cheering for most of the game. When Terrence Ross made that steal in the fourth quarter, it was the loudest I had ever heard that arena. I thought the roof was going to blow off.

And then, on the next possession, Kyle Lowry's game-winning shot attempt was blocked, and suddenly, the season was over. It was silent for five seconds, and then the fans gathered themselves and applauded the team for an incredible season. This group of guys had brought the Raptors back to relevance.

Now, you see Raptors fans everywhere. Detroit. Cleveland. New York. Portland. Los Angeles. Orlando. At almost every road game, there are huge contingents of Raptors fans in the crowd. And they're loud. You can hear the "Let's Go Raptors" chants wherever you go. The Raptors have the best travelling fans in the league. They've come a long way. When the team first started, they were a joke on the road. Nobody wanted to watch them play.

To think we went from those early years at the SkyDome to a large contingent of Raptors fans being at the very last game in Oracle Arena for Game 6 of the 2019 NBA finals. I didn't think anyone outside the Bay Area would be able to get a ticket to that game. But there they were, fans decked out in Raptors gear in the lower bowl, cheering, being loud and demonstrative. And near the end of the game, they outcheered the Golden State Warriors fans in the building.

I knew this day would come, but could I have imagined the fan base would grow to this extent? No way. A lot of credit goes to the franchise as well. They're good guys on the court and a team run by nice men. Fans feel connected that way to guys like DeMar and Masai.

The Raptors fan base is truly a cult, but a friendly and supportive one, if that makes sense.

7

INTERNATIONAL PLAYERS

Since its humble beginnings as an NBA expansion franchise in 1995, the Toronto Raptors have always brought a bit of international flavour to their roster. Now, has it always worked? Not really. But it sure made for some entertaining characters and moments.

The very first Raptor to sign a contract with the team was Vincenzo Esposito. This wasn't like the Los Angeles Lakers landing Shaquille O'Neal, or the Miami Heat signing LeBron James, but the hoopla was just the same.

Because of his Italian background, the press conference to formally introduce Esposito to the media was held at the Columbus Club in Little Italy. From the very start, the Raptors were conscious of the different pockets of ethnic neighbourhoods they could appeal to, and the Columbus Club was a very popular Italian social club with an old-school feel, and certainly the signing of Esposito brought a sense of pride to the community.

You could say the introductory presser was the highlight of Esposito's time with the Raptors, which lasted a whole 30 games (also the entirety of his NBA career). When the Raptors announced his signing, I had never heard of Esposito before. Having covered international basketball tournaments, I was familiar with foreign players, but only those who actually had a bit of buzz before they were considered for the NBA.

Bev Smith was one of the top basketball players in Italy, and I called her to get an impromptu scouting report. She was certainly not as high on Esposito as Isiah Thomas was. Sitting at the Columbus Club watching the press conference unfold, nobody was certain whether this guy was going to be good enough to play in the league, but it was sure a good marketing ploy.

There aren't too many on-court memories of Esposito's time with the Raptors. At the very first practice in Hamilton, I was with Chris Young of the *Toronto Star* and I remember him telling us, "Look, I don't know if Damon can play, but I know Vincenzo can't." He couldn't shoot well enough or create for himself. He wasn't even the best player from Italy. Before his brief tenure with the Raptors ended, though, there was one fun moment.

The Raptors were playing the Atlanta Hawks at the SkyDome, and whenever Esposito checked in, game ops would play these Italian tunes to really ham it up. One time he was checking into the game, the music blasting through the stadium speakers, the crowd cheering for him, and Steve Smith, a guard on the Hawks, was completely bewildered by the whole scene.

He looked at Esposito and said, "Who the fuck are you?"

Vincenzo replied, "I am Vincenzo."

And that was the very first Raptor to sign a contract with the team.

Even though not every international signing panned out, there was a purpose to what the franchise was doing. The Raptors as an organization has always made a conscious effort to reach out and find players overseas because I think they believed that foreign players would be comfortable in Toronto. Here, in a sprawling metropolis surrounded by people of all backgrounds, including their own, the guys could speak their own language, hang out with their own people, and find a home away from home.

In my opinion, Toronto is one of the best cities in the NBA for European guys. It might not work the same in cities without our culture. It was another strategic thing, too. If American players had their own reservations about playing in Canada, well then, the Raptors said, why don't we go and find equally talented players from overseas who actually want to be here?

It was a way for the team to get a leg up when it came to recruiting international players. Nowadays, when you look around the league, there are talented foreign guys on almost every team. The reigning Most Valuable Player is Giannis Antetokounmpo, better known as the Greek Freak. The best player in the NBA in five years might be Luka Dončić, who hails from Slovenia. Back then, it was a bigger deal. There was a stigma towards foreign players: They were too soft. They wouldn't be able to adapt to living in North America. Slowly, those stereotypes would go away, and today, the game of basketball is truly global.

Truthfully, I've always found the international guys more fun to be around. Because I had covered plenty of Olympics and World Championships, I was able to relay those stories to them. They were fun to chat with, and far more worldly. You could talk to them about their experiences growing up in their own countries. With American players, they've often gone a more traditional route. They would play for an AAU team, then for a Division I NCAA school, and then make their way to the NBA.

The paths were much different for international players. If I had to make a list of favourites, José Calderón would be at the top of the list. Calderón left his family as a teenager to play basketball professionally in Barcelona and eventually made his way to the Raptors. Through conversations with him, I came to learn that he was part of a pig farm co-operative back home, and that this co-op produced some of the best jamón in Spain.

For some reason, the jamón could not be imported to the United States directly, but you could ship it to Canada, so Calderón actually became the jamón connection for players around the NBA. There was one time after the Raptors played the Portland Trail Blazers when fellow countryman Rudy Fernández came strolling into the Raptors locker room. Calderón handed him this package and Fernández ran to catch the team bus. I asked Calderón what was in the package. He said, "Doug, you can't tell anyone, but you can't get this jamón in the United States." Calderón was not just the all-time franchise leader in assists on the court, but also off of it. A jamón trafficker, as it were.

Calderón was also solid in restaurant recommendations. There's this place in Mississauga not five kilometres from my house where he used to take teammates and visiting opponents for dinners, because while it was nominally an Italian bistro, the chef at the time was from Spain and, according to Calderón, made the best paella outside of that country. Sure enough, I went there one time, dropped Calderón's name, ordered the paella, which wasn't even on the menu, and it was outstanding. That's the kind of recommendation we'd never get from a North American-born and -raised player. The international guys had an interest and a breadth of knowledge they got from expats in the city that helped everyone out.

The franchise's biggest free agent signing was also an international player. In the summer of 2009, the Raptors landed one of the most sought-after free agents in Hedo Türkoğlu, who was just coming off an NBA finals run with the Orlando Magic. Paired with Chris Bosh, the Raptors thought they had a duo that could lead them back to contention, but Türkoğlu's tenure was just as short-lived and as much an afterthought as Esposito's.

Türkoğlu played a total of one season and 74 games with the Raptors and was an utter disappointment. The team missed the play-offs and traded him to Phoenix for Leandro Barbosa in the off-season. He was an expensive mistake for the Raptors to get rid of. They'd signed Türkoğlu to a five-year deal with $50 million plus.

People always ask what went wrong. To me, it was pretty simple. On the one hand, Türkoğlu was someone who liked to have fun. He wasn't a very hard worker when he was here and he loved the life-style of being an NBA player. He would hit up the clubs every now and then and never really took the basketball thing all that seriously once he signed the big contract.

The Raptors coddled him, and from training camp, it set the tone. They gave him training camp off and he never really got back to the level he was at in Orlando. He liked being an NBA player, but I don't think he liked the work it took to be an NBA player. Just like Esposito, though, Türkoğlu got his own introductory press conference. They had a busload of young Turkish students come in and made a huge deal out of it.

But if you want to talk about the most memorable introductory press conference for an international player? My dark horse pick would be Mengke Bateer. The presser was held at Pacific Mall in Markham, Ontario, on a Saturday, and they had hundreds of Chinese kids there for the occasion. I'll never forget it because my son, who was four at the time, was there, too. I still have the picture framed. It was on the front page of the *Toronto Star* sports section, a photo of Bateer surrounded by hundreds of Chinese kids, and somewhere in there is this white, blond-haired kid. My son.

I could go on about the international players who have come through Toronto. We all remember Andrea Bargnani, even if it's for the wrong reasons. Croatian Roko Ukić? I remember he would tell us all the time, "You have to come to our country, it's not like Toronto, the women are gorgeous there." Uroš Slokar was an interesting guy. He was super into computers and open-source management, that kind of thing.

Linas Kleiza was another guy who didn't really take the basketball thing too seriously, but thought very highly of himself. He always made a point of making a big show of who he was. One time, we were in the locker room, and he called me over. "Doug, keep it fair, keep it fair," he said over and over again, making sure I would write something nice about him. "Write me up good," he said, flashing a roll of American bills at me. Towards the end of his tenure here, the Raptors were going to buy him out, and the news broke in his homeland of Lithuania. I wondered who broke the news. "There's these two girls," he told me. "They come to Toronto all the time, and I always tell them shit I shouldn't."

There are so many other names I could mention. Primož Brezec. I'll never forget him. During every time out, Brezec would make a point of going to the scorer's table and stretching his legs even though he was never getting much playing time. It was just part of his schtick.

Jorge Garbajosa, who could have been a really great player here if it wasn't for injuries. When he was with the team, the Raptors played pre-season games in Italy and Spain. Garbajosa and Calderón were huge stars back home. We were in Madrid, and I was at the team hotel, the Weston Presidente, with my colleague Steve Buffery when we met for a beer at the hotel before going out for dinner. Garbajosa was across the room with his agent, spotted us and our beers, came over, and ordered us some new beers. "That one you are drinking? It is for girls, too light. You must drink this." He was right. It was called the Presidente and it was delicious.

One of the things we came to appreciate about most of the international players was their view of the world—basketball and societal—and of where they fit. Garbo was probably the best at one-liners that showed just how he saw himself. And those around him.

There was one game-day morning when FIBA, the world governing body of basketball, had named Garbo that year's Mister Europa, the same day the NBA had announced he'd won the league's Rookie of the Month award.

As he was leaving a shootaround, I sidled up to him and said, "Hey, congrats. Mister Europa and Rookie of the Month, big day for you." Without a beat, he turned and said: "If I am the Rookie of the Month, this league is fucked." Love a guy who doesn't take himself too seriously, and it always struck me that the European Raptors were leaders in that regard.

One other Garbo story. We're in the locker room one night before a game and Jim LaBumbard, the head of the team's media relations department, was chatting with Jorge and me. Jim was dressed as he always was on game days, shirt and tie and very businesslike, and Garbo called him over.

"Jim," he said quite seriously, "if you wear that tie in my country, you will get beaten up." It was apropos of nothing, but it speaks to the fact that the non–North Americans just seemed to be more comical, more conversant, more open to bigger things than their traditionally raised teammates.

There were plenty of international players throughout the years, most of them memorable for all the wrong reasons, but the whole approach to finding players of diverse backgrounds has paid off in recent years. You only need to look at the 2019 championship team. Marc Gasol from Spain. Serge Ibaka from the Republic of Congo. Jeremy Lin, an Asian American born and raised in California, who was the idol of Asian fans worldwide. The team was built by Masai Ujiri, a Nigerian, and Bobby Webster, whose mother is a Japanese American from Hawaii. The Raptors were Canada's team during the championship run, but they were also truly a global team.

Of course, we can't forget about Pascal Siakam, the kid from Cameroon who played a huge part in helping the Raptors win their first title and seems destined to be the face of this franchise for years to come. On draft night, when his name was called, we had no idea who he was. You figure, as the 27th overall pick, maybe he would eventually develop into something, or else he would just become another forgotten-about selection late in the first round.

In Siakam's rookie season, I remember Dwane Casey came up to me pretty early on and said this kid was going to be okay, that he was going to be a pretty good player. But nobody could have seen this coming. He was the D-League finals MVP in 2017. Soon he was a staple in the Raptors rotation. Siakam was named the Most Improved Player in 2019 and was an all-star starter in 2020. The sky's the limit for this kid.

After all these years, the Raptors have finally found their international star.

8

THE CHARACTERS

The Raptors have made a conscious effort over the years to find as many "good guys" as they can to fill the roster: non-controversial sorts, good people who've comported themselves in a perceived right way. They've been overwhelmingly successful in that pursuit; it is to their credit that they've had few knuckleheads.

But a few bad apples and odd sorts have slipped through the cracks, and it started in year one.

You have to understand that the first-year team, with the notable exception of the foundational piece in Damon Stoudamire, was dotted with reprobates and players very much on the downside of their careers, with bad contact and suspect or much diminished skills who were basically unwanted.

The very nature of the expansion draft to stock the team ensured that. Each of the other 28 teams could only lose one player and got to protect its top eight. It left the pickings slim, and Toronto's last two picks turned out to be two of the biggest "characters" ever to wear the uniform.

John Salley, the 25th of 27 picks—Toronto had to take 14, Vancouver had to take 13—had maybe the most tumultuous three-month stint of any Raptor ever, and he jazzed up that first season for us like no one else.

I should probably put it this way: Salley was far more interested in having fun at that point in his career than he was in playing for a dead-end expansion team.

People loved the idea of a big-name NBA player from their city— and Salley was a recognizable name after being in the league for nine seasons. His happy-go-lucky nature resonated with fans and with us—he was a good quote and good storyteller, too. He'd been with the "Bad Boy" Detroit Pistons and he'd chat with us whenever we needed it.

He "hosted" a New Year's Eve party that first year, but the party didn't turn out quite as well as anyone would have liked. It was at a club on the water at Ontario Place, one of the hot areas for clubbing in those days. Security was lax, to say the least. The coat-check area was staffed at the start of the night, but as 1995 turned to 1996 and John Salley's party raged, the coat-check staff abdicated and people walked away with whatever jackets they wanted at the end of the affair, about the same time as some overserved soul somehow plunked a car into the lake.

When we asked Salley about it, he denied all responsibility, saying "The party just had my name on it, I wasn't going to go." That was one of our first introductions to how NBA players would gladly lend their name to an event to either help a buddy out or make a few bucks, but accepted no responsibility for what went on.

And Salley's departure was just as memorable. We were out on a West Coast trip—I was writing about Steve Nash at Santa Clara

University as well as covering the Raptors—and late one night, Bill Harris of the *Toronto Sun* and I were having a nightcap in the lobby bar of the Fisherman's Wharf Marriott, the same hotel the Raptors were staying in. About midnight, maybe later, we notice Salley at the desk, his bags packed and checking out, and, intrepid reporters that we were, we chased him out of the lobby to his waiting limo to find out what happened.

"I'm done," he said of the waiver process that had set him free. "Tell the people of Toronto that I love 'em."

Quite a guy, Salley, quite a three months.

But of all the characters, none was more difficult, more cantankerous, more central to a handful of ridiculous stories than Oliver Miller, a jumbo-sized expansion draft pick up from the Detroit Pistons who was crucial to one of the more outlandish events ever.

There was what came to be known by beat reporters who followed the team—okay, me and Billy Harris—as the Drinking to Forget Tour. It was a four-game trip at the end of the 1997–98 season that ended with a disastrous 16–66 record, the darkest year in franchise history.

Why did we drink? Why was it memorable? The story?

Sure.

The trip begins in Atlanta where, predictably, the Raptors lose, and during one time out, Oliver Miller is goofing around with the Harry the Hawk team mascot instead of paying attention to coach Butch Carter. Well, that ticks Butch off. It also gets his brother, Cris, hopping mad and he's ready to challenge Miller to a fist fight outside the team's locker room before cooler heads prevail.

Next it's off to Washington for an off-day and the two of us plus Butch and one of his assistant coaches are lined up to take a limo to

Camden Yards in Baltimore to watch the Orioles and get away from everything Raptor for a day. Plus, Boog's BBQ beyond the right field wall is to die for.

We're in the hotel lobby, packed and ready to go, when Butch comes down to tell us that he's sorry but we can't go because we have to work. They've just suspended Oliver for a game for conduct detrimental to the team, and Butch thinks we have to write a big story. We write a note, maybe four paragraphs, and are in the car by 4:10.

The next day, they lose to the Wizards, of course, and the intrepid reporters are off to Philadelphia, a short train ride or easy drive from D.C., right?

Wrong.

Somehow, and I never did get to ask the travel agent how, we end up flying—WITH A STOP—and it's bizarre. We get up in the air, the plane turns right, we land in about 10 minutes, and more passengers get on. It's pouring rain—teeming—and I look up from my seat, which is about 7A (both a window and an aisle seat), to see the flight attendant patting Billy's shoulder with a towel because the plane's leaking, and she's saying, "I'm sorry, sir. This shouldn't be happening."

Well, it was. We take off again, turn left, fly for about another 10 minutes, and land in Philly. We get out of the plane, race directly to the store in the airport, and buy a map. It's only then we discover we've had our stop in Salisbury, Maryland.

It's a day game in Philly, there's a 100 percent chance we're hungover from a night in the lobby bar, and as we're sitting in the room across from the locker room where the coaches do their media stuff, we see Oliver Miller being wheeled out of the Raptors room on a stretcher.

Something about chest pain and they're being careful and transporting him to some hospital. Details are a bit sketchy, and as we're sitting around the coaches' room with a bunch of staffers and writers, the great, great Phil Jasner of the *Philadelphia Daily News* says, "Don't worry, where they're taking him has the best cardiac unit in the city, he'll be fine."

And then, the line:

Without missing a beat, Butch Carter says: "If they find a heart in that [bleep], tell 'em to take it out."

Spit takes all around. They lose that game, lose a night or two later in Milwaukee, and we're so beaten down and worn out, I remember nothing about it.

But the story lives on forever.

That was high comedy that played out over a week, but the number of one-off, one-time stories are too many to count.

Percy Miller was, frankly, a basketball *suspect* more than a prospect, but he was also the rapper Master P and he had his dreams—dreams the Raptors and coach Butch Carter wanted to make come true, as fanciful as they might have been.

Miller arrived at training camp in October 1999, the same time he was on the cover of *Fortune* magazine, touted as one of the wealthiest Americans under 40 years old, net worth of somewhere around $350 million US, the guesses were.

"My whole dream was to be a basketball player, be in the NBA— and this music thing blew up for me," Miller said at the time.

Truth was, his basketball skills were dwarfed by his music skills, but as much of a hoops oddity as he was, he was famous; and in 1999, the Raptors courted fame because they were hardly a talented team.

There was a pre-season game in Dallas, at the old Reunion Arena, and our seats were courtside right near the bench. "P," as he was known, hadn't played and probably wasn't going to until a group of savvy fans along the baseline started clamouring for him, chanting, "We want P, we want P" until Butch relented and put him in the game. It was quickly apparent that he was overmatched. His career might have lasted about another week before the Raptors mercifully released him.

"He was crushed," Vince Carter told us.

But the Raptors got some notoriety out of it, and at that point in the franchise's history, notoriety was at least as important as any on-court success. Music and basketball weren't as deeply tied together then as they became in the 2010s, and truth be told, a Canadian-born and -raised writer starting out on the beat like I was had no clue who Percy Miller was. Soon found out, though.

No story about the characters who have come and gone—the players who ran counter to the franchise's desire for talent combined with good character—could possibly be complete without a tale or two about the one and only Rafer Alston, known as the street ball legend Skip to My Lou for his ball-handling wizardry, playground acumen, and an over-the-top personality that simply did not mesh with the NBA, or the Raptors.

Skip was a handful, headstrong and opinionated—he'd call out teammates for their failings, he was supremely confident in his own abilities, and he always thought he deserved more shots, more minutes, more responsibility.

It came to a head one night in Boston during yet another lost Raptors season. He and coach Sam Mitchell—who was as headstrong as Skip himself, maybe more so—got into an argument on the bench after Skip got a technical foul or did something that pissed off Sam. Alston was banished to the locker room for most of the second half.

He was waiting for us after the game, and we appreciated that a lot because many players in similar circumstances would have fled the premises. But there he was.

He proceeded to tell us that he was frustrated, not at all enjoying himself, and that he might just walk away from the astonishing six-year, $29 million contract the Raptors had given him because, as he said, "Maybe the NBA and I aren't made for each other."

To have an NBA player admit he might quit and leave a king's ransom on the table was jarring, and as we digested that tidbit, we moved over to apprise Jalen Rose of it.

"That's strong," said Jalen.

That Jalen didn't go further was a brilliant piece of restraint, because if we're talking about "characters" over the first 25 years, the relationship between him and Skip would be central to that aspect of franchise history.

Put bluntly: They didn't like each other.

I don't think either respected the talents of the other; each always thought the other guy thought he was better than he actually was and, as teammates, they mixed like oil and water. Not well.

It did provide a night in Charlotte like I had never seen before and haven't since and never will, I am sure.

They spent an entire game not passing to each other. Seriously. If a play call meant for the ball to go from one to the other, there had to be an intermediary. Jalen passed to Chris Bosh who passed to Rafer. Rafer passed to Alvin Williams who passed to Jalen. Incredible, and in our courtside seats, I remember looking at Alvin as he checked into the game and saying, "What the fuck is going on?" And all he could do was shrug.

No one ever admitted publicly what had happened and there never were any repercussions outside of a couple of guys saying, "What the hell can we do, it's Jalen and Skip."

Jalen was, I'd say, the most underrated of the quotable players in the history of the team and seemed always to have a quip and the ability to make a point.

In his last season he lost his spot in the starting lineup, and that meant something to him. We knew it, so we made a beeline to his locker after the game to see what he had for us. We stood there silently waiting for him to get dressed. Shirt, tie, slacks, socks, jacket, shoes, earrings, on they went as we waited.

"Jalen," he was finally asked, "what do you think of the move?"

"Well. Look at me. It's a funeral, all in black. Right down to my drawers," he said, showing us that, yes, his underwear was indeed black.

The best, though, and this is absolutely undisputed, was Charles Oakley.

He was irascible but kind-hearted, opinionated, and more than willing to share those thoughts. He didn't care what you thought and would always speak his mind no matter the situation.

He would rant and rave about "young kids" in the game in those early days of the 2000s, how it was "all about the hype" and they were too soft, all the while sitting there knowing his teammate Vince Carter was one of the most hyped players in the game. But Oak didn't care and I love him for it, to this day.

And in the 25 years I've been around the team, he provided the single best quote I've ever heard. Apropos of nothing because that's how Oak operated. He didn't care; sometimes I don't think he thought about what he was saying, he just said it.

He got suspended for a game one time, and the first chance we got to speak to him about it was the next night in Cleveland before the game. We huddled around his locker, and Rob MacLeod of *The Globe and Mail* asked him: "Oak, do you think you let the team down by getting suspended?"

He looked up, smiled: "The NBA let the team down by putting it in Canada."

What? We were stunned, of course. I couldn't figure out what he meant, none of us could, so we let him ramble on about "hype" and "kids these days," and the original expansion agreement and I can't remember what else.

And then he dropped a line on us I will never forget.

"Pimpin' ain't easy, pimpin' ain't dead. Hos are just scared."

Jim LaBumbard, the media relations guy at the time, was standing behind us. He clapped his hands and said, "Okay guys, scrum's over."

We raced back to the work room, baffled. We had no idea what Oak meant, it had no context in anything we had talked about, and we had no idea how we'd get it in our papers. "Hos" was not something the *Toronto Star* wrote about in those days.

We never did figure out what he meant. I once asked him and he just laughed and said, "I don't know either, just something I wanted to say."

Oak, man. There will never be another.

Since early in the franchise's existence, it has been the goal—an honourable goal if often unachievable—to have rosters populated by good people, good citizens, men who would do the team proud with how they comported themselves away from the game.

And for the most part, the Raptors have succeeded. The vast majority of players who have worn the uniform over the years have been good and honourable people. Perhaps not the most loquacious, and maybe they rolled their eyes at some of the misperceptions about them and their craft, but generally good people.

For the most part.

There have certainly been some, um, different characters over the years, difficult characters, characters who played into whatever stereotypes people might have wrongly had about them.

They might be outliers in the grand scheme of a quarter century of basketball here but, in the early going and the lean years, they provided some crazy stories that could have threatened to undo what good was being done.

And it started right away, like in year one.

So while it's nice and lovely that in the 10 or so years of their first quarter century, the Raptors were lauded for being good guys who were in it together and for the greater good, the early years provided more than a couple colourful characters and stories.

For years, when I'd be asked what the Raptors were really like to cover, I had one standard answer I'd offer up.

"They're a far better story than they are a team," I'd tell people.

The various characters made it that way.

9

CANADIAN PLAYERS

When the Raptors joined the NBA in 1995, Canadian basketball was a bit of a wasteland. The national men's basketball team wasn't very good, so there was no buzz about them. It was the same bunch of guys who would get together for two weeks whenever there was a tournament and get their brains beaten out. There was also no cachet to wearing the Team Canada jersey, which has been an issue for as long as I've been covering the game, a troubling issue because I truly believe that some of the best experience any world-class athlete will have comes from representing his or her country. In the United States, representing your country meant you were part of all-time great teams like the Dream Team, who dominated the 1992 Summer Olympics in Barcelona. Everyone on that team became a rock star. It couldn't be the same for Canadian athletes because of economies of scale, but it'd be important not only to them but to those who want to be like them.

As much as the Raptors needed to develop into an NBA power-house, so basketball in Canada needed to grow. The progress has been immense over the past two and a half decades. And so much of it can be attributed to the fact that Canada was awarded two NBA teams in 1995. The first wave came from the sheer fact that young kids growing up in Toronto would now be able to go to the SkyDome and watch the best basketball players compete against each other.

In those early years, Kelly Olynyk's dad, Ken, worked as an assistant coach with the Toronto Raptors. He was the head coach at the University of Toronto and had a close relationship with Glen Grunwald. As a kid, Olynyk would hang around the team often. There's even a photo of him with Vince Carter. Kelly's mother was the first-ever scorekeeper for the Raptors.

The connections don't stop there. Cory Joseph used to come to games as a high-schooler. Tristan Thompson grew up watching the Raptors. Just having a team here was instrumental in pushing a lot of kids towards basketball who otherwise might have only viewed hockey or other sports as options. It takes 10 years to develop a pipe-line of players, and that's what having the Raptors in Toronto did.

From early on, the Raptors would occasionally try to bring in a Canadian player, guys like Rowan Barrett, who played for Canada at the 2000 Sydney Olympics and became the general manager of the national senior men's team. None of them were ever good enough to make the team, though. It felt like a token position: "Here's our token Canadian guy." He would play a few games in pre-season and then not make the team. It might have been tokenism but I still believe it was important just for kids to see and realize that they, too, could one day play for the Raptors, or for any other team in the NBA. The more kids who got into basketball, the more chances you had of them turning into good players. It trickled down and the Raptors even invited Canadian kids in for private pre-draft workouts; we all knew it was a long shot that many of them would ever play high-level professional basketball anywhere, let alone in the NBA, but the message the Raptors were sending was clear: we'll help develop the game and give kids something to shoot for because it's important for the sport.

The second wave came when Vince Carter was drafted by the Raptors, revived the franchise, and became *the* most exciting player in the game. The Slam Dunk Contest. The dunk over Frédéric Weis at the Olympics. The playoff run in 2001. The Vince Carter effect on basketball was very real. I still remember back in 1995, in my neighbourhood in Mississauga, you could walk down the street and barely see a single basketball net on the driveway. Today—and it started to change early in the first decade of the 2000s because of Carter—there's a hoop at the end of every other driveway it seems; that's the overall impact the franchise has had on the development and growth of the sport.

By 2000, after Carter had captured the imaginations of kids across the country, you could see a hoop on the driveway every third house. Times were definitely changing. I don't even remember having seen a road hockey net in the past 15 years.

At the same time, Team Canada had its own moment at the 2000 Summer Olympics in Sydney. They were led by Steve Nash, a point guard from Victoria, B.C., who had been taken 15th overall by the Phoenix Suns in 1996. He was approaching his prime and would go on to win back-to-back MVPs.

At the Olympics, Nash captained Team Canada to several signature wins. In the round robin, they upset Spain and then stunned a stacked Yugoslavia team. Nash dominated that game, scoring 26 points with eight rebounds and eight assists.

Heading into the elimination round, momentum was building for Team Canada to potentially medal. But they lost a close game to France in the quarter-finals. It left Nash in tears. They rebounded and beat Russia to finish seventh. When Nash spoke after the tournament, he said, "Hopefully, kids in Canada will be inspired to play . . . that's what I really hope."

Even more than the 1983 World University Games gold medal game, when an upstart Canadian team beat a United States team that included Karl Malone and Charles Barkley, that run at the Sydney Olympics helped spawn a generation of Canadian talent.

Canada is now the second-biggest producer of NBA talent behind the United States; in the 2019–20 season, 24 Canadians appeared in NBA games, and it's almost no longer something we take notice of. Back in the early days of the Raptors, we celebrated the odd Canadian as an anomaly—Nash, and Rick Fox, and Bill Wennington were outliers. Today, a Canadian-born or -trained player is hardly newsworthy. I honestly wonder if many of those kids who now play in the league would have dedicated themselves to the sport if they hadn't seen teams like that 2000 Olympics squad, or even the run-of-the-mill NBAers they could go watch in person in downtown Toronto.

With the combination of the Olympics run and the success of the Raptors, things were looking up for basketball in Canada. Then Carter left for New Jersey and Team Canada failed to replicate the success of their 2000 run. The momentum of basketball in Canada stalled a bit. Coincidentally, over a decade later, it was Nash again who could have revived the Raptors.

It was the summer of 2012, and Nash was a free agent. He was no longer in his prime but still a top-tier starting point guard. His brilliant run in Phoenix was coming to a close, and now he was looking to end his career with another team. The Toronto Raptors made a push to recruit him in free agency. Nash was very close to coming home, and I think he would have been a good fit. It was down to the Raptors or the Lakers.

The Raptors didn't want Nash just because he was Canadian. It would have been great from a marketing standpoint, but I think Nash was also intrigued by the possibility of helping to revive the dormant Raptors. But for many reasons, some of them personal, Nash chose the Lakers. You probably still remember the *Sports Illustrated* cover of Nash and Dwight Howard in Lakers jerseys.

It didn't work out in Los Angeles for Nash. He broke his leg in his first game with the team and never really got fully healthy after that. A lot of Raptors fans look back at it in hindsight and say the team dodged a bullet. I get where they're coming from. After all, their Plan B was acquiring a point guard named Kyle Lowry, and you know how that turned out. But I think Nash would have been good here.

It would have been a monumental moment, too. It would have been a smart basketball decision, and not just for the sake of parading a Canadian player on the roster but because of Nash's stature in the game, a two-time NBA Most Valuable Player. It showed, in a way, how far basketball had come in Canada. The Raptors wanted him because he would help the team, not because of his nationality.

The talk about bringing a Canadian player to the Raptors didn't end there. Before the team started their current run of post-season appearances, there was a lot of talk about dismantling the roster and tanking for Andrew Wiggins. Lowry ended up staying in Toronto because James Dolan got tired of getting fleeced by Masai Ujiri and the team was galvanized by the Rudy Gay trade. The We the North era was born.

The tanking for Wiggins thing was real. I never understood that approach at all. When you tank, it takes so long to get bad, and then twice as long for you to get good again. You also have to hit everything right on your way up. Look at the Philadelphia 76ers. Joel Embiid and Ben Simmons are cornerstone players, but even they are flawed and there were so many mistakes along the way. And they still haven't made it past the second round.

Also, I'm not sure Wiggins has the personality to be *that guy*. It would have been a horrible failure.

I always thought the first Canadian star to play for the Raptors had to be ready. Not everyone is built for the homecoming narrative. In my opinion, Anthony Bennett made the worst decision coming here to play for Toronto. He probably didn't have much of a choice, because he had struggled as the number-one overall pick in Cleveland. But here, the attention is always on you when you're Canadian. People would ask every day why he wasn't playing; it couldn't have been easy for him.

Cory Joseph became a Raptor, too, but he wasn't a star, only a role player off the bench, so there were fewer expectations for him. To be here as a Canadian, you have to have a strong personality. It's hard to play at home. There's a lot of pressure. Will they ever get *that guy*? I don't know. These days, you look around the NBA, and it feels like there's a Canadian player on every single team.

The Raptors have a tradition now of welcoming back Canadian players as they come through at the Scotiabank Arena with their own jumbotron tribute. It feels like we have one every single game. Guys like Jamal Murray and Shai Gilgeous-Alexander look primed to be superstars in the game. But will they want to come here and be *that guy*?

Better yet, do the Raptors still need to have a Canadian star on their team? I don't think so anymore. They're so good now, they're one of the best organizations in the NBA. They don't need to parade around guys just because they're Canadian. They just won a championship. A decade ago, landing Nash would have been a big deal. Now it's just, Can he help them win? and not, Is this player from Canada?

If the Raptors joining the NBA was the first wave, and the Vince Carter era was the second wave for Canadian basketball, the third wave would be the championship season. Now, even more kids want to be basketball players. The last two decades have been great in establishing a pipeline, and now you have five-, six-, seven-year-old kids who just watched their favourite team win a title. Like the previous waves, you won't see it manifest for another decade, but I bet in 10 to 15 years, you're going to hear a number-one draft pick from Canada talking about how he was at the Raptors championship parade and it made him want to hit the basketball courts, get in the gym, and get better.

It would be a pretty damn good legacy for this championship team.

Things are looking up for Team Canada, too, and the intersections of the Raptors and the national team are stronger than ever. Nash is involved with the team, and he's *the guy* when it comes to building relationships with Canadian players around the league. He is RJ Barrett's godfather, and guys like Murray and Gilgeous-Alexander have talked about working out with him.

Glen Grunwald is part of Team Canada, and truthfully, he's been one of the steadfast supporters of the national program since he joined the Raptors. His desire to see the game grow in this country has been consistent throughout the years—it has never changed.

Nick Nurse is the coach of the national team program, and I think that gives the team a certain level of cachet, too, to have a coach with an NBA championship leading them.

I think Canadian basketball is in really good shape, and now they need to succeed on the world's biggest stage. If they could bring home an Olympic medal, it would inspire another wave of basketball players in this country. There's enough talent now; it's just a matter of getting a commitment from all the guys, to ask them to feel pride in representing their country, to take the time to do it. There are a lot of factors to it: money, life, family, schedules, free agency, injuries.

Two decades ago, playing for Canada didn't matter. I think that's slowly starting to change now. But it still takes a group of guys to make it happen, to pave the way for everyone else. Guys like Olynyk and Joseph are always up for representing their country, but we need buy-in from everyone, especially when you look at the talent pool now.

Even with Nash's success in the NBA, he still talks about the Sydney Olympics as one of the best experiences in his basketball career. I wish more Canadians would compete at these events. They're missing out on a once-in-a-lifetime experience.

If Team Canada ever wins an Olympic medal? It would be on par with an NBA team coming to this country. We've come a long way, both the Raptors and the national team, but there's still plenty to do to continue to grow the game of basketball in this country.

10

MEDIA AND ACCESSIBILITY

A lot has changed in the 25 years of covering the team. The biggest change over the years? Players are much savvier and smarter now, and in the age of social media and with publications chasing click bait, players want to control the message more than ever.

Nothing encapsulated this more than when Norman Powell came to do his usual scrum with the media at the practice facility earlier this season. I was standing in the back, and when Norm came over, I joked and told him, "Say something outrageous." *Help us out. Give us a nice sound bite to work with.*

Norm looked at me and said, "Trust me, I'll never say anything that becomes a story." When I asked why, he explained that the one time he did, it was back when he was a UCLA Bruin and the team lost in the NCAA tournament. And in a moment of frustration, he told reporters that if head coach Ben Howland was coming back, *he* wouldn't be coming back. The story made headlines, and Norm vowed to never be put in that position again.

I don't blame the players. They've seen a lot of their friends get burned. There *are* a lot of unsavoury people out there with the *gotcha* questions. But what I miss about the disconnect now between the media and players is the relationship building. Having been around the game, I pride myself on being able to have a conversation with these guys, even if we come from different backgrounds and don't have the same interests.

You used to be able to walk into a locker room before the game and just shoot the shit with guys. The locker room is opened for 30 minutes before the game, and now, within that period, everyone is either stretching, having dinner in the private area, on their phones, or all of the above.

Back in the day, I would just walk in and be able to strike up a conversation with Antonio Davis, or even Vince Carter. In the very, very early years, I would always chat it up with Damon Stoudamire and Popeye Jones. We would talk about anything. Popeye remembers when the famous rapper The Notorious B.I.G. was gunned down in 1997. We were in the locker room processing that.

Nowadays? Chit-chatting with Kyle Lowry before a game?

Good luck. Some players still do it but they are very much in the minority. It's partly because they legitimately have other pre-game routines to take care of—physical treatments from the training staff, consistently scheduled on-court workouts—but some of it is that they just can't be bothered. They don't see an upside to the chit-chat, they don't need it, it does nothing for them, so why do it?

Players used to care about what we did, too. These days, they don't give a shit. Chauncey Billups used to live at the SkyDome hotel, and I would be a guest on *The Reporters* on Sunday. There were a few times when I would pop into the locker room on Sunday afternoon, and Chauncey would be like, "Doug, I saw you on TV."

They still read what some of the beat guys will write, but not as much when they have places like *The Players' Tribune*, where they write their own stories. There was accountability, too. You knew that if you ripped someone, you had to show up and face them.

One story I remember about this is when Keon Clark stopped talking to me for two weeks. I was talking to Keon and Frank Zicarelli of the *Toronto Sun*, and Keon just looked at me and said, "I'm not talking to you." I was bewildered. Was it something I wrote? I asked him for what reason. "You know," he said. "I don't know," I told Keon. He just said, "I'm not talking to you. Fuck it, get out of here."

I went to Jim LaBumbard and asked him what was up. He just said even he wasn't sure what perceived slight had made Keon stop talking to only me. To this day, I'm still not sure what I said. Maybe they were playing an elaborate prank on me. Either way, two weeks after, things just went back to normal and Keon and I talked again.

That's the only time I can remember a player specifically singling me out as the reason he stopped talking to the media. And, frankly, I didn't care all that much; it wasn't as if my stories were going to suffer much without the odd comment from one player on the periphery of the team.

Whether it's good or bad, being around the players allowed you to build meaningful relationships, some that would last over the years. The players also become more trusting with you. Privately, they'll tell you stuff. It might not be earth-shattering or even something you'd want to report right away, but those private conversations might yield stuff that can augment a story a week or two down the road. Those little snippets turn into bigger stories as you develop them from an original tip, and it's all part and parcel of covering a team on a daily basis.

The players know it, too. If you work the beat well, you develop trust and relationships and open lines of communication that are there when you really need them.

Or when they really need you.

Morris Peterson, one of my all-time favourites, totally understood how the game was played and how we could help him in ways no one might understand.

Mo had lost his starting job at the beginning of the 2005–06 season to rookie Joey Graham and it wasn't sitting well with him.

We were in the locker room when the player with the locker two down from Mo—I cannot remember precisely who it was—was holding a post-game scrum. I was about three people deep in the scrum, right at the back, and basically standing in Mo's locker. He saw me and started whispering in my ear: "Doug, this has gotta change. I'm pissed. I gotta get my job back, this isn't working."

He knew I'd keep his name out of it, he knew he was getting to a writer who'd do a fair job and do it in a way no one would know. I pretended to be listening to the scrum while holding a conversation with Mo over my shoulder, and I got a pretty good story out of it that was mine because I'd built up the trust with Mo by being around all the time and treating everyone fairly.

It's important. Very important. And it only comes with the access that we need to do our job well.

I will say, over the years, the team generally had good guys, especially star players like Vince Carter and DeMar DeRozan, Chris Bosh or Damon Stoudamire. I can't think of any time any of them absolutely blew off the media. We might not need them every night and they appreciated that night, but those four specifically would talk after practice, after shootaround, after games whenever we needed. They might not say anything too newsworthy but they would stand there and talk. That's very much a Raptors thing; it doesn't happen with the best players on every other team, but the Raptors have always been accommodating, or at least the top players were. I think the team's various media relations bosses—John Lashway, Jim LaBumbard, and Jennifer Quinn chief among them—have impressed upon the best players the need to work with the media rather than against it, and it's been to the benefit of all.

There are always exceptions, good and bad. Andrea Bargnani was a boring kid. Joey Graham was really self-serving. Rafer Alston could be prickly but he was entertaining. And Jalen Rose was the most underrated quote ever. He always had a story for you.

Jalen used to always tell us that he was working towards "being a part of the media," too, so that's why he fed our appetite for stories and the quotes that drove them. He was on the cutting edge of a new NBA phenomenon that's developed over the last decade: the ex-player as writer/broadcaster. When we first started, the media and the players were two very separate entities. They played, we wrote about it, and seldom did the two mesh. As the media grew, and became a 24/7 beast that needed to be fed, more and more players and coaches became crossover stars.

They'd get their own shows, their own columns, and their own profiles as commentators. Even guys who could be standoffish with reporters found out they could make some money, extend careers, become experts that people wanted to hear from without the filter of a reporter or a broadcaster. I've always felt that this spoke more to the audience than it did the players. People want to hear from the horse's mouth, so to speak.

Oliver Miller was just a bad guy. I remember in our first year, something happened; we reporters went and talked to him after a game, and he told us we were on probation for three weeks. Charlie Lemmox, a reporter with Broadcast News, replied, "We still get paid, right?" We did and no one suffered by not hearing pearls of wisdom from Oliver Miller for a couple of weeks.

We've had our share of coaches, too.

Brendan Malone was really patient, especially because he had to teach a lot of us about the little things, as even the reporters were learning basketball. He would go out of his way to point out the minutiae of the game, like footwork on pick and rolls, watching the off-ball stuff. Post-game, he would say, "This guy had 30 points and here is what he did well. He did all of these things well, but the two other guys made it happen by setting the screen." Brendan was a big teacher, and he found a lot of willing reporters.

On the other hand, Lenny Wilkens was very condescending. He would never engage in conversation with us. But you could never shut Sam Mitchell up. Kevin O'Neill was always prickly. Generally, coaches don't like to be questioned on their strategy, and as a reporter, you have to know how to deal with it.

You can't be confrontational and ask them, Why did you do this? Now, you have to be more careful and have conversations with them, as opposed to just hitting them with the hard questions. People say, Why don't you ask the hard questions? Well, if we ask them the questions the way fans want every day, you're going to lose them for weeks, if not longer. My biggest thing in talking to players and coaches if there's a big story is whether or not it's worth losing a guy as a source for this one story. Generally, the answer is no. To me, no story is that big. At least not one that I've come across yet.

I miss watching scrimmages from back in the day, too. I think it was on the insistence of Isiah Thomas and Glen Grunwald, but every full practice was opened, and you could pop in and watch them. I've seen more three-man weaves than I care to see for the rest of my life. Some people needed it, and they had to teach the media so they could teach the people.

I miss watching these guys play basketball. Nowadays, they open the last half hour of practice up to the media. Back then, though, you would watch not just drills, the three-on-three, sometimes five-on-five scrimmages. The access has eroded over the years. The half an hour rule is just a lip service rule.

The behind-the-scenes back-and-forth with a team's front office is interesting, too. The day before the Raptors were going to trade for Jermaine O'Neal, they had a free agent camp here before summer league and a bunch of us went to the Harbour Sports Grille afterwards. We had a table in the back. Wayne Embry, Sam Mitchell, Bryan Colangelo, and the rest of the staff were there. I was one of the few writers there. Bryan came up to me and said, "Come sit next to me," and we got to chatting. He said, "I know you're not a big fan of JO." I said, "I'm really not." And he told me, "I'm gonna trade for him but I need some help." He said, "It can't come from me. Do you have anyone in Indiana?" Bryan needed plausible deniability, pure and simple. He didn't want me to be the only guy with the story because everyone could figure out where it came from; if there were two reports, no one could be sure where it originated.

I called Mike Wells, then the Pacers beat writer for *The Indianapolis Star*, this was a Saturday afternoon, and Bryan said the deal would be done on Monday. He said if I could get someone to write the story with me, I could publish it at ten o'clock.

I called Wells and told him a TJ Ford for Jermaine O'Neal trade was happening. He checked with Larry Bird, who confirmed it off the record, and we got our stories done and were going to put them up on our websites at the same time. We would both hit the button at 10 a.m. But he published it seconds before, and everybody started the story with, "The *Indianapolis Star* is reporting . . ." That kind of pissed me off, but I understood how things worked and quickly got over it. Those who knew, knew what was what.

The one year Masai Ujiri redid Dwane Casey's contract, Masai texted me and said, "Case is done. Three years. [X] dollars." I beat the great Adrian Wojnarowski of ESPN by a minute. I remember someone asking how I'd got that, because beating Woj did not happen with any regularity. I checked my phone before him, which is the only reason why. That's what the media is like now.

The U.S. media market is a huge deal for players who play for the Raptors. They enjoy the attention of the major outlets. It can make you feel a little bit second rate. It's not an anti-Canadian thing. I'm fine if ESPN writes a giant feature that's better than what I could do. I totally understand that. But the day-to-day stuff, I'm going to win those. My readers are going to be well served.

It's harder now. The level of competition is so huge; if *Sports Illustrated*, ESPN, or *The New York Times* writes a huge feature, I don't feel like I can match it, because if I write a similar story after, people will say you're just piggybacking on that guy. Getting stuff first is a big deal, too, but I don't care about that anymore. What does first mean now? First is like a three-minute advantage over someone.

Writers are competing with players themselves, too. When Kyle wrote a *Players' Tribune* feature, we said, "Why didn't you tell us?" and he was just like, "I'm not telling you shit." I don't have a problem with players telling their own story, but they also don't have to answer for it. They'll write something and it becomes a two-day story. There's no accountability. They get to tell their side of the story as they do without anyone being able to question them or challenge facts or draw out more information.

I've always worked on this basis: most "interviews" are simply conversations that yield information that the public wants to have. It's never the first question that gives you your story; it's always a follow-up or a different line of questioning that gives you your story and it only comes from a normal conversation.

Maybe I'm the only one, but I still think the media can play a huge role in telling stories about the players and the team these days. Now, if only the players will let us into their world again.

11

VINCE CARTER I

It has been a complex relationship that's existed between Vince Carter and the Raptors, and their fans and the game of basketball across Ontario and Canada as a whole. He is, without question, the most astonishing athlete to ever play for the Raptors; at the height of Vinsanity, he was one of the most popular athletes on earth, and he took us on an incomparable ride for his six-plus seasons with the Raptors.

It is a story with three distinct parts—an improbable beginning, a tortuous, elongated departure, and finally, redemption. It was made of incredible highs and devastating lows, and for as long as there are Raptors, Vince Carter will be central to the narrative. As well he should be.

And to think it all happened with some help from Dallas Mavericks boss Don Nelson.

The night of the 1998 NBA draft in Vancouver was a rather ho-hum affair. The big story was that local hero Steve Nash was momentarily on the stage to make the selection for the Phoenix

Suns, but he disappeared just before the proceedings began, traded from the Suns to the Dallas Mavericks, and all of us there to chronicle the draft were totally tied up in that transaction. It was *the* story for basketball in Canada, so when the Raptors chose Antawn Jamison fourth, we hardly blinked an eye.

We'd heard they had some interest in Jamison and his North Carolina teammate Carter, so not only weren't we surprised by the selection, we weren't all that taken aback by the trade that sent Toronto's pick of Jamison to Golden State for Carter, who the Warriors had selected one spot later. We weren't sure why the draft had gone down that way, but it didn't matter. We had a Nash story to deal with.

Leave it to general manager Glen Grunwald to explain it and describe Don Nelson's role.

"They [Golden State] were afraid we were going to trade with Dallas. Nelly always lied so much I don't know what he was telling them, but we knew that they didn't like Vince Carter, so . . . they were concerned we could trade with Dallas, Dallas would take Antawn Jamison, and we'd still end up with Vince Carter. They really wanted to get Antawn Jamison, and that assured them the draft selection of Antawn Jamison. I don't think it was true, I don't think we had any real discussion with [Dallas] about it. I think they were always after [Dirk] Nowitzki, which turned out to be a pretty good pick. [The Mavs traded their original pick, Robert Traylor, to the Milwaukee Bucks for Nowitzki, an unheralded shooter from Germany who turned into the best player in Mavericks history.] We did okay, too."

Did they ever.

Carter's time in Toronto was a wonderful whirlwind of dunks, fame, wins, excitement, and a buzz never before associated with the

Raptors. His rookie season began late—a lockout reduced the season to 50 games and it didn't begin until February 1999, but when it did start, it kicked off the most exhilarating era we'd ever seen.

Carter made the Raptors "brand" a worldwide phenomenon during his time in Toronto and gave the franchise a cachet around the basketball world that it had never had. He turned the team from something of a running NBA joke into a global entity; he was that famous. That gifted. That good.

The individual dunks, the game-winning plays, the highlight-reel performances are almost too many to recount.

There was a game-winning dunk one Sunday afternoon over the imposing presence of Houston Rockets Hall-of-Famer Hakeem Olajuwon. There was one that Carter tells me to this day is among his favourites, a dunk over Atlanta's shot-blocking force Dikembe Mutombo that Vince punctuated with a finger wave, the Mutombo trademark. In his second game as a pro, in Indianapolis, he threw down a double-pump, twisting baseline dunk that had us all thinking, "This kid's something special." He was fluid and graceful and could be powerful in anything he did on the court. It's trite to say it was effortless because it's the last thing it was; it took work and dedication and determination and innate skills few mortals have.

I was in awe of some of the things he did, and I saw almost all of them over the years. The period from the NBA All-Star Weekend in February 2000 to the Olympic Games in Sydney that September was almost indescribable.

Carter cemented himself at that point as one of the top 10 basketball players on the planet, and it was an incredible journey to be on.

Oakland and the All-Star Game was one of the highlights of the first quarter century of the team's existence. It rained the entire weekend there, it was that gloomy, and the bus rides from our San Francisco hotel through the jarring, maddening traffic over the Bay Bridge to Oakland dampened everyone's mood, pardon the pun. The dunk contest had been on hiatus the year before as the NBA tried to "reimagine" it when all it seemed to need was this other-worldly athlete in that purple and black Raptors jersey.

His performance was singular. There have been better "competitions" like Michael Jordan vs. Dominique Wilkins and Zach LaVine vs. Aaron Gordon, but never before and not since has one player dominated a night like Carter did that evening. He went through the legs and behind the back after taking a bounce pass from his cousin and teammate Tracy McGrady; there was a 360-degree windmill dunk; and he hung onto the rim by his gawd-damn elbow. Astonishing.

We were sitting at the far end of the Oracle Arena, great seats if a bit far away, and our jaws dropped with each dunk. You could feel the wave of noise in the building after each one, and we all turned immediately to the television monitors in front of us to make sure we'd seen what we just thought we saw. To this day, it's hard to describe the emotion at the performance, the way it enthralled us. The way Carter enthralled us.

It was the same later that year in Sydney at the Olympics. The Canadians were caught up in our own national team and its run to the quarter-final, but Carter was never out of our sight or our mind. I was in the arena the day they played France and saw something I hadn't seen before and haven't seen since. His dunk over the seven-foot Frédéric Weis of France was jaw-dropping; he left the floor from just inside the free-throw line, elevated over the defender, and dunked. It was one of those moments where there was almost silence in the arena after it happened while the 18,000 or so fans processed what they had seen. They couldn't believe it. And the gasps that eventually came, the screams and yells and cheers, were something I will never forget. I saw Vince Carter do a lot of amazing things—that moment will resonate forever.

And if you don't think the entire world noticed, how about this from LeBron James in a 2015 interview. James was a six-year-old kid at the time he heard about it: "All I remember was hearing people like, 'Did you see Vince Carter jump over a guy in the Olympics?' I was like: 'What do you mean he jumped over a guy? Like, was he laying down on the ground?' When I saw it, I was like, 'Oh my god!' That's the one play where you knew he was like, 'Half-Man, Half-Amazing,' for sure. You were like, 'Oh yeah, that nickname is too fitting.'"

Carter also guided the Raptors to their first playoff appearance in 2000. From the moment he showed up in Toronto and gave us a glimpse of his otherworldly talent, everyone knew it was only a matter of time before Toronto would take the next step on the court.

There wasn't a huge celebration when the Raptors finally clinched a playoff spot. They were in Indianapolis when it happened late in the regular season. Matt Akler, a member of the team's media relations staff, crunched the numbers about 90 minutes after the game, and we all realized they were mathematically in. Many fans and people in the organization had waited many years for this moment. Perhaps it felt anticlimactic. Perhaps it was because we had started to expect greater things from this team beyond just a playoff spot with Carter as their star player.

The first playoff series wasn't much of a celebration. Back then the first round was a best-of-five series, and the Raptors drew the

New York Knicks, an experienced team with championship aspirations. Toronto lost the first two games in New York and returned home to host their first-ever post-season game. The games were close, but when Larry Johnson banked in a three-pointer at the top of the key late in the fourth quarter of Game 3, Toronto's season was over.

Carter's first playoff appearance was a learning experience. He struggled the entire series against Jeff Van Gundy's defensive schemes. The Knicks game-planned for Carter and took him out of the series. There was a whole different level of attention being paid to him whenever he was on the floor, and Carter forced the issue a bit with his play. He wasn't able to be himself. But the three-game sweep would give him a bit of resolve to come back stronger the following season.

The Raptors lost Tracy McGrady in free agency to Orlando that summer, but Carter continued to grow as the team's centrepiece, and they returned to the playoffs, with another matchup against the Knicks for the first round. All eyes were on Carter to make up for his previous post-season run, but through the first three games, he struggled from the field again. The Raptors trailed 2–1 heading into Game 4 at Air Canada Centre.

The pressure had intensified. Carter had done so much for the franchise and the city of Toronto, but now the conversation had shifted to whether he could lead this team in the playoffs. Carter stepped up in Game 4 to help the Raptors even the series, and then helped guide them to a series-clinching win in New York in Game 5. It was a seminal moment for the franchise—to win their first playoff series on the road at Madison Square Garden. At the mecca of basketball. It was a huge deal.

Finally, it felt like the Raptors were a relevant team. That was the first major step towards legitimacy for this franchise. Getting into the playoffs for the first time was fun and unique, but winning a series, a hard-fought series against a battle-tested team like the Knicks? That was a pretty bold statement.

As a person dealing with a media horde that was unimaginable for a basketball player in Toronto at that time, Carter was complex. He loved the game and didn't really love the adulation. He grew tired of talking all the time, but talk he did.

Whether we needed him post-practice, post-shootaround, post-game, he would stand and answer the questions. He might not say much that was worth reporting but he'd say something, and for a lot of the media, that's all they needed, the sound bite, the smile, the presence.

He'd get tired of some questions and could bristle at them. "I ain't dunking no more," he once said in a moment of frustration, and while the saner among us knew that to be not true, it became a story. He had a sore knee, and reporters would call up doctors who'd never seen him for their take on his injury. "A knee is just a knee," he once said, and that became a cause célèbre because we couldn't figure out what he meant.

Carter would also have to deal with some of his older teammates, who had no problem calling him out in public. One guy who always held Carter responsible was Charles Oakley. Because of his experience in the league, whenever Oakley spoke, his words carried a lot of weight.

Oakley was never afraid to call his teammate out publicly. He used to call Carter the captain of the ship, the pilot of the plane. Carter was their meal ticket. Alvin Williams used to joke to me that his job was to throw the ball to Carter and get the fuck out of the way. Because Carter was so talented, Oakley and the other vets on the team were especially demanding of him. Taking care of him also meant holding him accountable.

I'm sure there were times when Carter wished Oakley would just shut the fuck up. It probably hurt Carter to hear his teammates question his toughness and wonder if he had the mental makeup to be the number-one guy on a contending team, but privately he understood those questions. Now, years later, Carter talks about how much those veterans helped him grow as a player. He gives all the credit to those guys for moulding him into a better player.

Carter once told me years and years later that he didn't really enjoy the constant media attention but he understood his responsibility to do it. So he did it. He had this guy, Peanut, who was part minder, part bodyguard, part body man, and Peanut was the designated stopper. If he got this look from Vince that meant no more interaction with the people, there was no more interaction with the people.

Vince could be overwhelmed when he was out in public, and I think we all understood that enough was enough and the man deserved some peace if he wanted it. He wasn't standoffish, as such, he just grew tired of the constant adulation. We'd see the crowds gathering outside road arenas before and after games just to cadge an autograph or a picture, and they were everywhere. It could be tiring but it spoke to what Carter was and what he was making the Raptors into.

Many times, this discussion would rage and it was a legitimate question: If, in 2000 or 2001, you put Carter and Toronto Maple Leaf great Mats Sundin at opposite ends of the Eaton Centre, which star would draw the biggest crowd? It was the first time I truly thought that a basketball star could equal or even eclipse a hockey star in popularity. Carter was that big.

He made the Raptors more famous around the globe than they ever were. It had been a long time since Toronto had a superstar in any sport who was at the level of Carter. We always feel like we need validation from the rest of the world, and here was a guy in a Raptors uniform who everyone was talking about.

He was a privilege to cover and to be around; it was like being on the periphery of Beatlemania in some ways. I used to tell him that he was not only making himself world famous, he was helping us carve out a level of notoriety because we got to write about him all the time and watch what he did. Parts of a beat grunt's job can be mind-numbing and difficult and not at all fun; knowing that Carter might do something we'd never seen before or would ever see again was the very best part of the gig.

And if you got close enough to him, you really got caught up in it, as I did in the final few months of his time in Toronto.

12

VINCE CARTER II

It didn't end well for Carter in Toronto, and I thought that was truly a shame because of all he'd done for the franchise, the city, the country, and the sport.

In the last 20 games of his Raptors career—at the beginning of a 2004–05 season that followed two straight years of missing the play-offs—Carter posted career lows in most statistical categories and was accused—I say unjustly—of checking out on his team.

Being labelled a quitter is the worst possible indictment for a pro-fessional athlete; it is not a charge any reporter should throw around lightly, and I thought it was unfair to Carter.

Yes, his role changed. The franchise saw Chris Bosh, who came aboard in the 2004 draft, as its next star player and was transitioning to Bosh as the focal point of the offence, which cut into Carter's role, his prominence, and what everyone had been used to from the still-young star.

He knew it, too.

I was out at a local establishment one September Wednesday night, hanging with my pal Steve Buffery of the *Toronto Sun*, when my cell phone rang.

"Doug? It's Vince Carter. Got a minute to talk?"

I was, understandably, dubious.

"Sure, I do. Gimme your number and I'll call you in half an hour, just out having a beer." It's an old journalistic test: if it's really some unexpected caller and there's no way to confirm, buy some time to check. Besides, I was on a stool next to a competitor, and the last thing I needed was Beezer listening in on my conversation.

The caller said he'd phone me in half an hour, which was fine because it'd give me time to check things out. I called Raptors media relations Jim LaBumbard and said, "You'll never believe this, somebody pretending to be Vince just called me."

"Um, Doug? That was Vince. He called me to get your number because he wanted to talk."

Holy shit. This kid better call me back, I can't screw this one up.

Sure enough, he did, in precisely half an hour. I excused myself from Beezer, then stood in the bar's parking lot with my notebook on the roof of my car as Vince proceeded to tell me, "Maybe it's time to go. It's just time for me to look after me."

I told Beezer something had come up and that I had to go. Then I raced back to the *Toronto Star* offices—I didn't routinely carry my laptop with me back then and there was no such thing as typing a fast story on a phone—and filed the story, in time for the second edition, that caused the predictable uproar and set the wheels in motion for a memorable start to an interesting season, the first under rookie head coach Sam Mitchell and neophyte general manager Rob Babcock.

From that day on, it was inevitable that Carter's time would soon come to an end. He backtracked a bit as the season began—he talked to assistant coach Micah Nori the night before he was dealt about maybe coming off the bench, perhaps changing the playing rotation so things could be worked out. It was a bit of damage control because even if Carter truly loved and appreciated Toronto for what it meant to him, the team was changing, he was changing. Things change.

And they did forever for Carter and the franchise, for Rob Babcock, and to some degree for Sam Mitchell as well on the night of December 17 in Indianapolis.

We got word of the trade while in the arena at about four o'clock and we were dumbstruck. Vince Carter—VINCE FUCKING CARTER—got traded for a bag of deflated basketballs. Aaron Williams (37 games in Toronto), Eric Williams (62 games in Toronto), Alonzo Mourning, who was never coming in the first place and everyone knew it immediately, and the draft pick that would become the eternally disappointing Joey Graham for Vince Carter.

We stood there in the hallway trying to process it. In the 20 games he played that season in the Raptors uniform, Carter only averaged his Raptor lows in points (15.9), assists (3.1), rebounds (3.3) and, most important, minutes (30.4). He took fewer shots per game (15.1) than in any other season with the Raptors, and that's not entirely on him. I remember thinking as those 20 games unfolded that maybe it was time to go. I just didn't think he'd go for such a cheap return.

Neither did the great Jalen Rose, who never met a conversation he didn't want to join until he walked by us that evening on the way to the locker room. "Guys," he said in that twangy Jalen voice, going into his third-person persona, "for the first time in his life, Jalen is speechless."

And somehow, the lopsided trade became Carter's fault. Go figure.

He was vilified as few ex-Raptors ever have been; the venom and hostility and outright anger and outrage that accompanied him on every trip to Toronto for almost a decade were unprecedented in team history.

None of the others—not Damon Stoudamire or Tracy McGrady before Carter or Chris Bosh after him—were treated with as much outward disgust as Carter was. I've always thought it was unfair and not commensurate with what he'd done for the team, the game, the Raptors.

I was tilting at windmills. I'd talk to him often over that decade or so when he was so loathed, and he'd always make the same point.

"It's okay," he'd say. "I know what happened, I know what went on. I still love coming here, that will never change."

From Carter's point of view, his frustration with the franchise was understandable. In his time here, there was never-ending turnover with the coaching staff and the front office. In his six years in Toronto, he played for four coaches and three general managers. Butch Carter coached him when he was drafted, then Lenny Wilkens took over. Kevin O'Neill had one nightmarish season here before the team hired Sam Mitchell. Glen Grunwald was the general manager who drafted Carter; he got fired, and Wayne Embry took over on an interim basis before Babcock took the reins of the front office.

The Raptors never found the right players to surround Carter with. Free agent signings like bringing in Hakeem Olajuwon at the twilight of his career didn't work. Management failed again and again to have the right mix of players to build a sustainable, contending team.

The instability and uncertainty wore on Carter. He was tired of it and didn't want to go through all of this again with a new coach, a roster that wasn't good enough, and a general manager he didn't trust.

The Carter trade would set the franchise back for half a decade. I couldn't believe they didn't land a single all-star for him. Even though Carter had taken away a lot of the team's leverage by making it clear he wanted out, you still would expect the Raptors to at least have gotten an all-star player in return.

Carter was under contract, and no matter how unhappy he was with the organization, the Raptors didn't need to rush into a trade. They could have waited the entire season if they wanted to. I think Babcock panicked and made a trade that did nothing for the organization. It also sent a terrible signal to the rest of the team. They knew after the trade that they weren't going to be competing for a playoff spot.

The bitterness of the Raptors fan base towards Carter only grew stronger immediately after the trade. As a member of the New Jersey Nets, Carter sat down for a much-publicized one-on-one interview with John Thompson on TNT. The main talking point that came out of it was how Carter admitted he didn't try as hard as he could have towards the end of his tenure in Toronto.

A bit of that was taken out of context. I give him credit for admitting it and saying it out loud, but I think Carter was also trying to say that he didn't do enough in the off-season to improve his game. People wanted to jump to conclusions that he'd admitted he wasn't trying in games, but it wasn't that. He recognized that even with his God-given talents, he could have put more work in his craft.

But no one in Toronto was trying to be rational about anything Carter-related at the time. Fans just heard what they wanted to hear, and it helped reaffirm the bitter feelings they had towards their former star player. I think fans held him responsible after the trade for management's failings.

Thankfully, the fans changed. It probably was because the Raptors had turned into consistent winners and moods had lightened, or fans simply got tired of hating someone they had once so loved, but about 2016 or so, peace was made. The night that Carter finally got his standing ovation as a video tribute played—a cathartic moment for him and the fans and the franchise—was truly emotional. I wasn't reduced to tears and neither was he, but it wasn't too far from that. There needed to be peace and love and memories of the best of times. It had to happen and it did.

There were even talks of him returning to play in Toronto the past few years, as Carter neared the end of his career. I was very much against it. It would have been unfair to him and the organization. The expectations would have been too great. There would have been too much focus on Carter, especially if he didn't play. It would have been a distraction, and knowing Carter's personality, he would have eventually come to resent it.

In the spring of 2020, Carter finally got to put it into words when we talked one night in Atlanta. "For me, I never felt that I should go out there and force people to understand me, my true love for the game. I just felt like it would happen organically over time, I just had to be patient," he told me as the last of his 23 seasons in the NBA was drawing to a close. "Time heals all wounds, but the approach that I chose to take, I preferred it be on their time. I knew I can't win the war in the media, I didn't feel like I could because of who I would be going against, so I just had to be patient, take the blows, be myself, enjoy it, deal with it.

"For me to come out years ago and try to dispute, fight against fans, people, outsiders, organizations, those who had this to say, I knew that's a lose-lose. I don't win and it wouldn't be a good decision. I didn't need any of my people around me to tell me that . . .

that made sense to me and it was a decision I chose. I'm personally glad I did it.

"I didn't have a timeline, I just wanted to continue to be myself, continue to love the game, continue to enjoy being on the court and competing, [and] one of these days, it will be okay."

I don't know how Carter will ultimately be remembered by the fans he so electrified for all those years. I don't know or really care that much how they felt about his departure or the shot that was inches too long that ended his most memorable playoff series—the 2001 Eastern Conference semifinal with Philadelphia that the 2019 series mirrored in so many ways. I don't know if the thought of Carter attending his university graduation the morning of that Game 7 still rankles as it once did.

What I care about, and what I try to make people care about, is the joy that Carter gave everyone for all those years, the plays, the dunks, the wins, the inescapable feeling that because of him the Raptors had arrived, basketball had truly arrived.

It was fitting, I thought, that Carter was in the arena in Oakland the night the Raptors won the 2019 NBA championship. He was there, sitting alongside his old teammate Tracy McGrady in their part-time roles as ESPN commentators, and it was nice, I thought, that he got to witness the franchise's ultimate accomplishment. That it was in the Oracle Arena, where 19 years earlier he had completed the dunk contest that fans will talk about forever, was just the pièce de résistance.

The moment was not lost on him, nor was it lost on any of us who witnessed his career and the team's championship. I asked him about it as his career was winding down, and he got a little wistful. "I just kind of made sure I thanked those guys, and I'm not big on doing it publicly but I did it," he told me of that night. "More than anything, I remember going down on the court, and the one guy I wanted to see more than anybody was Kyle [Lowry]. He was doing an interview and he wanted me to sit down and do it with him, but there was no way in hell I would do that. I know what he was trying to do and everything and I appreciated it, but this was their moment and it was cool to watch.

"It was cool to watch Nav Bhatia [the team's superfan and a close friend of Carter's family] live in the moment and to talk to him and all the other people around since that time. It was pretty amazing.

"I just wanted to be there to witness, I didn't want any of the shine of it. I just wanted to be part of the celebration like everyone else. I was just there to witness history. It was their moment," Carter said.

It was also a moment that had its genesis with him.

Vince Carter is the single most electrifying athlete I have ever seen on a constant basis, but he was more than that.

He was a franchise icon, a larger-than-life athlete, and a man for whom I have great respect.

He might not have been the best player to ever play for the Raptors, but he is the most important. I'm glad people understand that now.

One day, and I'm pretty sure it will be sooner rather than later, his number 15 jersey will be retired and hanging in the rafters here in Toronto.

The Raptors were lucky to have him for what he was as a player and what he meant for the game.

13

DEMAR DEROZAN

Seven little words typed in the wee hours of the morning, a quick comment on life, feelings, mood, and private thoughts, will be the lasting legacy DeMar DeRozan leaves not only on the Raptors but on basketball, on professional sports, on athletes, and the fans who demand so much of them, those who see them as entities rather than people with human emotions and the tugs of life that get to us all.

"This depression get the best of me."

It was on his Twitter feed during the NBA's All-Star Weekend in his hometown of Los Angeles in February 2018, and it sent shock waves through much of the fan base back in Canada. Emails and texts went back and forth through the night and into the early morning.

"Have you talked to DeMar? Did you check in with him? Is he okay? That was kind of dark." Between fans and reporters and then team officials in California, and then on to DeRozan himself, messages from those who knew him best and who wanted to reach out.

I was actually lying in bed—it was the middle of the night back in

Toronto—when the tweet first surfaced. One of my dearest, closest friends, someone who was a big-time Raptors fan with an affinity for DeRozan that was as deep as mine, first alerted me to it.

People say you should divorce yourself from social media or text and email conversations when the day is done, but in this instance, they were dead wrong. If I hadn't rolled over and checked the phone— as is common practice during the season when you're basically working 24/7—it would have been hours before I could even start the process of finding out what was going on.

I tried to reach DeMar to no avail, and sent texts to others I knew who were in Los Angeles for All-Star Weekend, like Dwane Casey and Jennifer Quinn, the team's media relations head at the time and an old colleague, boss, and a friend for two decades.

Yeah, he's okay, they said when they saw my questions, although he hadn't responded personally. Theories abounded: maybe there were family issues, maybe he was just toying with us, quoting song lyrics at the end of a long California night. He was DeMar DeRozan, for Christ's sake, he made millions, he was world famous, an NBA all-star, and a Canadian sports icon. What could possibly be wrong?

A week later, we found out.

The tweet, the comment, stayed fresh in the mind over the course of the next week. What did he really mean? What was really going on? Was he really okay?

The Raptors came out of the break with a home game on the Friday night, losing to the Milwaukee Bucks, but DeRozan had a typical game, 33 points in 41 minutes, the kind of production the team and its fans had come to expect from the favourite son.

The Saturday after was the first chance to talk, to really talk, and the opportunity to ask him couldn't be passed up.

The deal at Raptors practice at the time was players were paraded in front of a logo-emblazoned backdrop for scrums with however many reporters were present any specific day, and if anyone wanted a private conversation, it happened in a quick walk-off chat after the group session concluded.

This day was different, though. DeRozan wanted to talk, needed to talk, and when a private chat with a familiar face was arranged, it was in unusual circumstances. DeRozan wasn't going to do a scrum for the crowd; he'd talk to me but only away from the crowd, in the far corner of the practice facility, the team's locker room, a place few reporters ever get to see. He wanted privacy because he knew what the topic would be and he wanted it to be one-on-one. He didn't know what would come of it but he only wanted to discuss it with someone who'd been with him for years, someone he trusted because it was personal. Deeply personal.

"You know what was crazy?" he would tell me years later. "I never knew what would come of it. I don't think from that night when I made that tweet, if it wasn't for the relationship that we had, to talk freely and openly about it to somebody I felt comfortable with sharing something, I probably never would have spoken of it to nobody else. That's what helped me out. It was therapeutic to get it off my chest and talk about it with you. I'd be lying if I told you I knew what would come after it."

It was flattering to hear that but not too unusual. Of all the players to come through the doors over those first 25 years, DeRozan was the one with whom I made the strongest, longest connection.

It probably had to do with being around him basically every day of his first nine years in the NBA, watching him grow from a shy, quiet teenager into a confident man.

Many a day, after a practice or game, when the scrums were done and the minutiae of the evening or the day had been taken care of, DeRozan would stop to say hello, ask about the family and discuss his. The day my story about his tweet broke, the Raptors played. He, typically, played well with 20 points in an easy win over the Detroit Pistons, and the questions afterwards were centred on his story.

I had no idea what his reaction would be, whether my story went too far, got too personal, caused him too much bother. Players tend to want to talk about lesser things than their personal feelings, and he had crossed a line going public.

I was standing off to the side of the scrum, but he spied me when it was all over. I looked at him with one of those "You okay with that story?" looks and he said, "You da fucking man, Dougie. You da man. That was important. Thanks."

That's the kind of guy he was: he knew that it took two to tell that tale, any tale, and he wanted to make sure everyone was cool with it.

What came of it after was something astonishing. DeRozan had talked openly about the difficulty dealing with fame and real human emotions, and the immediate reaction to that conversation was, Man, this kid wants to talk, needs to talk, is going places athletes seldom go because they seem to be superhuman beings and to admit human frailties is somehow a sign of weakness. It's not right but it's a part of sports history: athletes aren't normal and can't suffer from real emotional issues.

"It's one of them things that no matter how indestructible we look like we are, we're all humans at the end of the day," he said that day. "We all got feelings . . . all of that. Sometimes . . . it gets the best of you, where times everything in the whole world's on top of you. This is real stuff . . . That's why I look at every person I encounter the same way. I don't care who you are. You can be the smallest person off the street or you could be the biggest person in the world, I'm going to treat everybody the same, with respect.

"My mom always told me, never make fun of anybody because you never know what that person is going through. Ever since I was a kid, I never did. I never did. I don't care what shape, form, ethnicity, nothing, I treat everybody the same. You never know.

"I have friends that I thought was perfectly fine, next thing you know, they're a drug addict and can't remember yesterday . . . I never had a drink in my life because I grew up seeing so many people drinking their life away to suppress the [troubles] they were going through, you know what I mean?"

He was okay with my story and I certainly was. I didn't know it would become as big as it did, but we would soon find out that it started a wave. The last story I wrote in April 2016 before losing a few months to some serious heart issues was about a group of Toronto kids who had put together their own book of supportive notes for DeRozan and had presented it to him before a Sunday night game against Orlando. He was touched, deeply touched, but I wasn't surprised by the gesture because I knew how deeply fans cared about him given all he'd done for the franchise.

There seemed to be some connection between him and the fans that was deeper than any I had ever seen in 24 years of covering the team. People *cared* about him.

Because of him, a handful of other professional athletes—notably Cleveland Cavalier all-star Kevin Love—opened up about their battles with mental health issues. In the aftermath of DeRozan talking openly about it, the NBA and National Basketball Players Association created confidential programs for players who needed someone to talk to.

For the DeRozan we all knew, it was a step out of the ordinary and a break with what some knew of him. He had always been open and forthcoming.

A total surprise, given what he was when he arrived.

One of the delightful parts of being around an NBA team for years and years is watching the maturity and the growth and the development on and off the court of teenagers who really don't know anything and have been dropped into a strange land among people they don't know. They come to us raw—mentally and physically—with great expectations and much pressure and are asked to immediately become men and to live and act as professionals.

It is not easy. It's in many ways an unfair ask of kids, but it's the way professional sports operates across the board, and only the very best thrive while the so-so might get by but eventually flame out. The woods are littered with the carcasses of "can't miss" players who miss entirely, youngsters who don't evolve and are gone in a relative blink of an eye.

These are teenagers, many of whom have been coddled by AAU coaches, high school coaches, university coaches, handlers, and street agents, and they immediately enter the cutthroat world of pro sports, where veterans protect their turf—and their paycheques—like hungry animals protecting their food.

They are not cut any slack. They have to perform immediately: teammates want to see what they've got, fans expect greatness far before the players are prepared to provide it, and the harsh reality is that if they fail, well, someone else will come along the next year, the next week, the next month, and it's see ya later.

It was that way on the night of Thursday, June 25, 2009, the evening of the NBA's annual draft, the selection of teens who are supposed to become saviours, and the Raptors were on the clock.

They had the ninth pick that night and were coming off yet another disappointing season, a 33–49 campaign that saw them miss the post-season for the fifth time in seven years.

Commissioner David Stern stepped to the podium as Raptors fans grew anxious, and in his inimitable and consistent fashion, he announced the selection of general manager Bryan Colangelo:"With the ninth selection in the 2009 draft, the Toronto Raptors select DeMar DeRozan of the University of Southern California."

Sitting in the team's draft-night work room, watching the proceedings unfold and getting ready to provide the kind of journalistic hot takes that are so often more wrong than right, the reaction was underwhelming.

"Who? The kid from USC? Oh, okay," was the general consensus.

It wasn't much more electrifying in New York, where DeRozan was when he learned where his new home would be.

"Canada? I don't know if I even had a passport," he recalled later. "All I knew it was cold."

Well, he knew a bit more than that. When DeRozan was a young lad growing up in Compton, California, in the early 2000s, he'd watched Vince Carter win dunk contests and energize the game, so he knew a little bit about the team and its dinosaur logo and its most famous player who had left half a decade before, but that was about it.

Toronto as a city? May as well have been Mars.

"No idea. None. Didn't know nothing about it. Knew it was cold."

And from such humble beginnings, legends are born.

To watch DeRozan morph from this raw, crazily athletic kid into one of the best old-school players in the game was a true treat. He came into the league like so many youngsters these days: a gifted athlete with no clue how to play professional basketball. He could jump out of the gym, as the saying goes, but had no clue about the nuances of the game: footwork on defence, how to create shots for himself and his teammates. Head coach Jay Triano, who thrust DeRozan right into the starting lineup as a rookie, used to tell us he saw so much raw talent in the kid from California it wasn't funny, and that when he learned to play, he might be special.

Everyone saw it. The Slam Dunk Contest of the 2011 All-Star Weekend, again in his hometown of Los Angeles, was a perfect case in point. He was by far the most athletic competitor. But he was robbed of the win when Los Angeles Clippers ascendant star Blake Griffin did a ho-hum job jumping over the front of a small car provided by an NBA sponsor while a choir sang at mid-court in a shameful bit of schlock that was unbecoming of the contest and the NBA.

That might have been the first time we all saw a publicly combative side to DeRozan, who again took to social media to express himself: "No more dunk contests for me unless it's in Toronto!" he said on his Twitter feed.

It was also the first time his great respect for and love of his second home became public knowledge, a characteristic that would make him unique among professional athletes who ply their trade in Toronto.

He loved the city because fans appreciated him for his abilities and very much let him live his life in peace, and he became an integral part of the franchise's ascension among NBA teams. His game improved almost every summer, ball-handling one year, shooting another year, recognizing defences being thrown at him and dissecting them another year. He was a diligent professional who strove to be better and to grow along with a team that became his own.

He had a unique way of connecting with the fans, as well. He, more than any other player, made sure the people knew how much he appreciated the support he got and the responsibility. Chris Bosh, who was the face of the franchise as its lone all-star when DeRozan arrived, left a year later, and DeRozan cemented his place in Raptors lore by tweeting out, "Don't worry, I got us."

He did. He became an all-star player, ushering in the start of the greatest era in franchise history. The win totals in the next eight years showed that steady growth: 22, 23, 34, 48, 49, 56, 51, 59. The post-season success mirrored that—rising from four years of no playoff appearances to five in a row, including a trip to the Eastern Conference finals in 2016.

It provided him with a lifetime of memories.

"We had so many but the one thing that started off was that first year we made the playoffs. I remember at the beginning of the season, there was so much that transpired, nobody knew what was going to happen with so much adversity, so many question marks, and we all just went out there and played and next thing you know, we started winning," he told me.

"We started winning like crazy, and to be able to go up against a Hall-of-Fame, veteran team like that Brooklyn team with a bunch of young guys and go seven games, man, that's one helluva story."

The day DeRozan left, that shocking July afternoon in 2018 when he was dealt away in a franchise-altering deal that brought Kawhi Leonard and ultimately an NBA championship to Toronto, marked a disappointing end to one of the greatest careers in Raptors history. DeRozan did not want to go, he longed to spend his entire career in Toronto, and there was much lingering bitterness from him towards team president Masai Ujiri for cutting him adrift. But those feelings of betrayal, and of loss, can't take away from what DeRozan meant to the Raptors and what Toronto meant to DeRozan.

He grew up as the franchise grew up, hand in hand, win for win, success for success.

It will be his legacy.

"I wouldn't take away from my time here, my experiences; the knowledge that I gained over my first nine years in Toronto won't change," he said early in 2019. "I'm grateful, I'm beyond grateful and thankful for the opportunities and everything that came my way. It shaped me into the player I am now and the man I am now.

"No ill intent or thoughts at all that I can think of. Shit, it's a helluva career if you just base it off my nine years in Toronto."

14

MASAI UJIRI

The first time I met Masai Ujiri in person was July 2007. At age 36, he was hired by general manager Bryan Colangelo as the director of global scouting. Colangelo had called me to say they had hired this guy from the Denver Nuggets and that I should meet him because he had a very interesting backstory. And so on a Saturday morning, I went to Ujiri's office at the Air Canada Centre to chat. It was the first of many conversations we'd have over the years, and it was illuminating.

I also had no idea I was about to talk to the man who would one day build a championship team in Toronto.

Ujiri came from humble beginnings in soccer-mad Nigeria, where he grew up in Zaria idolizing Hakeem Olajuwon and fighting long odds to even make it out of the country as a basketball player, let alone emerging as one of the top young minds in the game. But his story, one that was commonplace for young African basketball players of the time, was also a story of missed opportunity.

"When I played, you had to go to the basketball court between three and four in the hot, hot afternoon until the main players came," Ujiri told me in that first meeting. "When they came in, you couldn't play, there were only two courts. When it got cool at night, and the floodlights came on, the older, better players played. That affects the growth of the game because kids are not getting the right opportunity on the facilities."

I came away from that first meeting really impressed. Ujiri was this bright young guy who had a lot of big ideas and an infectious personality. His passion was obvious, and you could tell it was genuine. A lot of young executives would parrot company lines and subtly boost their own reputations; it wasn't that way with Masai that first day. You wanted to know him and about how he had travelled the world first as a player and then made it way up the NBA ranks as an unpaid scout. He would tell me stories about sleeping on couches of assistant coaches and scouts. You could tell that even now he was eager to keep improving.

He also spoke passionately about what he wanted to do in helping to develop the sport of basketball in Africa. It was and still is part of Ujiri's life work to make sure those opportunities denied to him are eventually available to all young African players. He hadn't had his chances, and he seemed bound and determined to make sure future generations weren't held back in the same way.

While his first task with the Raptors was identifying talent and nurturing it into something that would help the franchise, finding how to improve conditions throughout the continent of Africa was and will forever remain his passion.

It is something he began as director of the NBA's Basketball Without Borders program, something he continued as director of international scouting for the Denver Nuggets—a post he held until the Raptors came calling with that initial job under Bryan Colangelo—and something he'll go on pursuing into the future.

The byproduct is simple to discern: Ujiri's work and his dedication to a burgeoning basketball breeding ground like Africa cannot help but enhance the Raptors' presence there and, perhaps, allow them to unearth some gem.

"It's the unknown for now because of the lack of facilities and lack of coaching and infrastructure over there," Ujiri told me during our first sit-down. "The main thing about basketball in Africa is the kids don't start early enough because there is a lack of facilities. When they finally start at 15, 16, they are talented enough to come to college but they haven't been processed enough and they haven't played enough. That's why you see a lot of African players lack the feel for the game."

Ujiri developed his feel for the game in a journey that had many stops. He left Nigeria for prep school in Seattle, went to junior college in North Dakota and university in Montana. He played professionally in Greece, Germany, Belgium, England, and Finland, soaking up as much information as he could and adding to his list of contacts.

"When you're not good like me," he joked, "your agent has to keep getting you jobs in crazy places. It was a great experience for me, and that's what's helped me in the business because I ended up keeping a lot of my contacts. I thought it would be very helpful for me. You get to know coaches, basketball people around the world, and it all comes around."

In 2010, Ujiri would return to the Nuggets and get his first chance as an NBA general manager. At the time, Colangelo was sad to see him go from the Raptors but told me Ujiri needed to go and run his own team and have the experience of making his own decisions rather than just being part of the process.

The biggest challenge facing Ujiri in Denver was their star player Carmelo Anthony wanting a trade. In fact, he had very openly telegraphed his desires to become a New York Knick. It couldn't have been an easy thing for a first-time general manager to deal with, but Ujiri showed his fortitude and toughness by waiting things out, not panicking, and eventually getting the Knicks to sweeten the pot and put the Nuggets in a position to continue being a contending team even after trading their best player.

He was strong-willed and knew exactly what he wanted, and wouldn't do things on other people's timelines. He was willing to absorb some short-term pain and criticism in exchange for the long-term outlook of the organization. He wasn't a pushover; he stuck to his guns and aced the first big trade he had to make. Masai was going to comply with Anthony's trade request, but he was going to do it on his own terms.

He didn't give in to public pressure, and that impressed me from afar. It got the attention of the rest of the league, too. It was the first time we saw the resolve Ujiri had as the guy making all the decisions. It wouldn't be the last time.

In 2013, new MLSE president Tim Leiweke decided the Raptors needed a change at the top, and so Ujiri returned to Toronto on a five-year deal to take over for Colangelo—the man who first hired him—as the team's general manager. Leiweke identified Ujiri as the guy he wanted and was relentless in his pursuit to get his guy. He talked to Nuggets owner Stan Kroenke a bunch of times and discussed compensation in terms of money or draft picks.

It was flattering for Ujiri, too. He always felt a kinship to Toronto.

It was the NBA organization that gave him his first big shot. He knew the city and the organization and he wanted to come back and work for the team. A year before Ujiri would return and replace him, Colangelo was prescient, talking about what kind of general manager Ujiri was in Denver and would be in Toronto.

"When I hired Masai, I realized quickly he was very good at developing relationships and also exceptional at sizing up talent," Colangelo told me in 2012. "He was also very confident in his opinions on players and people and not afraid to express an opinion either."

From his very first day on the job, Ujiri instilled a pride in the organization, the fan base, and the city. He didn't buy into any of the crap about Toronto being an undesirable destination for players. He gave everyone a sense of pride and a "Fuck you" attitude to everyone else in the league.

"There is something about Masai when you get to know him as well as I do," said Leiweke. "I like to say he has the personality of a lion. He wants to be the king. I felt the same way about [Brendan] Shanahan and Kyle Dubas when we hired them [to run the hockey division of MLSE]. Masai went out and got Jeff Weltman and got Bobby Webster and the first person he hired was Teresa Resch. He knew how to build a culture."

Ujiri understood the culture and understood winning. He knew how much it would mean to this city and this country if they started winning. He saw greatness in the Raptors and the NBA in Canada. He always talked about the potential of having an audience of 36 million people.

"That's that big, bold spirit of his," was how Leiweke put it. "He's not afraid of making the difficult decision, and Larry [Tanenbaum, MLSE's chairman] desperately wants to win. You have to give Larry a lot of credit in this," he said. "When he first got here, Masai let a lot of good people go, 14 of them. It was a very, very hard thing to do. He doesn't make those kinds of decisions without considering every possibility. He has a big heart and a big conscience and he knew he was affecting lives, but he had to do it. He has the guts and intuition of a winner—and that's why he wins."

Ujiri galvanized the fan base. He stood in front of thousands of fans outside Jurassic Park and shouted, "Fuck Brooklyn" before a playoff game. It was a side of him we had seen privately—make no mistake, Ujiri is as competitive as they come—but for him to say it in front of thousands of people was shocking. He pushed back when Paul Pierce said the Raptors didn't have *it*. He was not afraid to put people on the spot and make bold statements. He told anyone who would listen that they would win in Toronto and that they would win big. He said it in his first press conference as general manager. He never stopped believing in it from that day on.

Ujiri wasn't just a loud voice. He could be calculated, ruthless, but most of all, he was a great team builder. Building a championship team doesn't happen overnight, but when you look back at the cumulative result of his roster moves, you can see a blueprint for how you build a title team over a period of time.

It started with parting ways with Andrea Bargnani, a first overall pick of Colangelo's who had come to embody everything about the disappointing Raptors. Ujiri knew Bargnani didn't have the mental toughness to win big. He was a talented young player but he wasn't going to be a central part of the team moving forward. Ujiri fooled the Knicks into trading for him and surrendering a first-round pick to Toronto in the process. It was a brilliant trade that helped speed up the process for the Raptors to be good again.

There was the Rudy Gay trade to Sacramento that helped jump-start the 2013–14 playoff push. Later, Ujiri made moves like trading Greivis Vásquez to Milwaukee in exchange for Norman Powell and a draft pick that turned into OG Anunoby. Moves like trading Terrence Ross and a first rounder to Orlando for Serge Ibaka helped nudge the Raptors closer to championship contention.

And then there was the Kawhi Leonard trade. DeRozan was a huge part of the family culture the Raptors had built under Ujiri, but that's the level of ruthlessness you need when the ultimate goal is to win a championship. Ujiri's thinking was clear: maybe we make this gamble and it doesn't pay off, but if we don't make it, we're going to regret it.

He understood he was going to take a public relations hit, and that it was going to cost him some goodwill with some of the players on the team. But he didn't care. If people wanted to be pissed, he could live with it as long as he made the best decision for the team.

Ujiri took all the playoff losses very hard. He knew it was a process and always tried to look at each playoff exit as a lesson the team had to learn. But he was always evaluating: What else do we have to do? Who do we have to bring in? What things can we get better at? Winning a championship is an obsessive pursuit, and there are a lot of setbacks along the way.

After the Raptors were swept by the Washington Wizards, Ujiri would have loved to just fire everyone the following day. But he didn't panic. He set those emotions aside and realized it wouldn't be easy. But the focus was always on what's next. How to get better. How to improve. He believed in the team. He also believed in himself.

Ujiri was also very smart not only in how he built the roster but in the hires he made in the organization. He understood that an

NBA team is basically a family and you need people who can get along. He wanted individuals who were not only good people but who were willing to listen to different viewpoints and be able to put aside their own opinions for the greater good.

You could say some of the front office people he's hired were inexperienced—Bobby Webster, Dan Tolzman, Teresa Resch—but they're also not ones to just say yes to everything. They'll give Ujiri their viewpoints, and while he ultimately makes the final call on things, he's not afraid to hear their opinions. In fact, he encourages them. He empowers those around him. It makes people want to work harder for him.

You also can't tell the story of Masai Ujiri without talking about everything he does outside of basketball. His Giants of Africa foundation and Basketball Without Borders will always be close to his heart. He feels a responsibility to the continent, whether it is new courts, basketballs, and shoes for the players, or bigger things like basketball camps and assisting with the education needs of young kids, teaching them about nutrition and respect for women.

Ujiri wants to pass on his experience and give the next generation the life skills they need, not just to become basketball players, but to be ready for the world when they grow up. He knows better than anybody that not everyone will become an NBA player, but perhaps they can become leaders in their communities, maybe as teachers, as doctors, or in business. Ujiri is all about giving kids more opportunities in basketball and in life.

Add it all up, and I think it's not outlandish to say Masai Ujiri is one of if not *the* most successful sports executives in Toronto sports history. In the 30 or so years I've covered Toronto sports, he's been the most consistently successful executive I've seen. Pat Gillick of the Toronto Blue Jays comes close. They won two World Series, but they were also really bad for a lot of years and never, ever had the global reach that Ujiri has given the Raptors.

The millions of dollars he's raised for the youth of Africa, the message of service to greater causes that he's given Raptors fans across Canada, and the message that winning is possible through consistent hard work and self-belief will be a legacy he can be proud of, a legacy the Raptors can be proud of, regardless of what they do on the court in the years to come.

When Ujiri does move on from the Raptors, they will miss his dynamic nature. There are a lot of smart people in the front office, but no one will come close to having the charisma and ability to rally an entire city, and entire country, like Ujiri has done. He's been the face of the franchise for almost a decade now.

When he's not here anymore, the next guy is going to have a really hard job.

Until then, in Masai we trust.

15

MAPLE LEAF SPORTS & ENTERTAINMENT

On the night the Toronto Raptors finally clinched their first NBA championship, I got a tad emotional watching Larry Tanenbaum—chairman of MLSE—celebrate with members of the organization.

Even before Toronto was finally awarded an NBA franchise, Tanenbaum always looked for any opportunity to bring a professional basketball team to the city. Tanenbaum was a construction magnate who'd turned his holding company, Kilmer Sports Inc., into a huge business entity that was very financially lucrative. He was also a huge basketball fan and a believer that an NBA team would thrive in Toronto. Baseball and hockey were taken, because of the Maple Leafs and Jays. There was no NFL interest back then. Tanenbaum saw the way that basketball could fit into the sports landscape here.

Starting in the late 1980s, whenever an NBA team was in trouble, there would be whispers of Tanenbaum trying to see if he could relocate them to Toronto. They included the Cleveland Cavaliers,

Denver Nuggets, New Jersey Nets, and San Antonio Spurs. Tanenbaum had his own way of doing business, and who could blame him, he was successful in everything he did, but the NBA is more than just a sports league, it's a partnership.

Because he went about it independently and never enlisted the help of commissioner David Stern and the league's front office, there was a bit of tension between the two sides. Stern read Tanenbaum the riot act, letting him know in very clear terms that this wasn't the way to go about bringing a team to Toronto. We have a process, he told him, and what you're doing isn't the process.

Tanenbaum never gave up. He was part of a group that put in a bid for what would eventually become the Raptors franchise. They lost out to Allan Slaight and John Bitove. I think those guys put forth a better business plan, but it might have been a little F.U. to Tanenbaum for all his manoeuvres before that. I know he was hurt to have not won the bid. He had done a lot of legwork. It was a passion of his. He wanted a basketball team in Toronto and he knew the market could bear it.

Stern used to always say that any kind of business, even an NBA team, is going to go through changes at the top, especially in the beginning. He always said the people who start with the business and guide it in the right direction aren't always the people who stand to see the end result.

The Toronto Raptors were a perfect example of that.

A few years into owning the Raptors, Slaight invoked a shotgun clause on Bitove. We were sports reporters, and not exactly the most well-versed in high finance and corporate dealings. All we knew was that this was a standard business clause, and now there was a deadline for Bitove to put together enough funds to buy Slaight out, otherwise Bitove would be bought out.

According to Glen Grunwald, Bitove was within $1 million of coming up with the money to take over ownership of the Raptors. It was a very tense night on the eve of the deadline. A bunch of us sat in this Italian cafeteria in the lobby of the building where the team had its office on Bay Street. At midnight, we sat and wondered who would win. It turned out to be Slaight. That meant the end of Bitove's run with the Raptors, and shortly after, Isiah Thomas's, too.

It soon became obvious that it made perfect sense for the Maple Leafs and Raptors to come together and operate under one umbrella, which we later found out was one of the wedges between Slaight and Bitove. Slaight, the radio magnate, knew the teams had to somehow join forces; it was the only logical business move and he pressed the point.

The Air Canada Centre was opening, and it made no sense for the two teams not to figure out how to play in the same building and operate as one. In 1998 the Leafs acquired the Raptors and formed Maple Leaf Sports & Entertainment (MLSE), with Tanenbaum, whose company had owned a small stake of about 12.5 percent in the Maple Leafs and Maple Leaf Gardens, brokering the deal.

But quietly, because that's his nature. Until he assumed the role of chairman of the board in 2003, taking over from Steve Stavro, Tanenbaum was very much in the background, just as he liked it.

The big worry everyone had with the two teams coming together was whether the Raptors would become a second-class citizen in the organization—that they would be the financial dreg, that the team didn't have enough cachet with the new ownership group.

The Leafs were, well, the Toronto Maple Leafs, and the Raptors were this brand-new basketball team that wasn't very good. Those concerns turned out to be misguided. The business people knew basketball was going to make money for them, and that's what mattered. There was a salary cap in basketball and costs were defined. It wasn't a case of starving the basketball side in order to pay the hockey side. Today, especially with the team's recent run of success, the Raptors are practically printing money.

The president and CEO of MLSE at the time was Richard Peddie. He was a very out-front guy. Peddie had run the SkyDome and managed major corporations, and he knew the world was changing and basketball was becoming more global. You would hear all these years about how difficult it was for general managers of the Raptors to get anything done, and that ownership and the board of directors would stall any plans for sustainable success on the basketball side, but that was simply not true.

Did the general managers have to make the case for spending more money to the board? Definitely. But most times, as long as it made sense, ownership would get on board. I don't know if the formation of MLSE saved the Raptors, but it certainly helped enable their success.

Peddie was a businessman who wanted to be in sports. He was very supportive of the people he hired in the front office but wouldn't hesitate to be hands-on. When you're running a multi-billion-dollar corporation, you need a guy to be hands-on.

Peddie was also a very staunch defender of Glen Grunwald, the general manager at the time. It was his idea to bring in Wayne Embry as a consultant for the team, which was a really good basketball move.

In April 2013, Tim Leiweke was named the president and CEO of MLSE. He brought a cachet and personality like we had never seen before in Toronto sports. Leiweke was loud, he was bombastic. The only thing bigger than his personality were his ideas.

He was really good at hiring people, and maybe he told us about it too often, but hey, it ain't bragging if you can back it up. It was Leiweke who tabbed Brendan Shanahan to run the Leafs and Masai Ujiri to take over as general manager of the Toronto Raptors. Those moves stabilized both franchises and were exactly what MLSE needed.

In bringing Ujiri into the fold, Leiweke identified a really good, young, promising executive with ties to Toronto. He went out, pursued it, and got him. The cost of business was letting incumbent general manager Bryan Colangelo go. Colangelo was a really good salesman and a knowledgeable business guy himself. He could get into a boardroom and convince guys that his vision was the right one for the franchise.

At one point, I think a lot of people here thought he might eventually become the next president of MLSE, but at that time, he was still very much a basketball guy. Colangelo had a lot of ideas himself for how the company could grow, but he wasn't in a position to put them in place.

Leiweke wasn't done there. He brought Drake on with the organization as their global ambassador. Leiweke had connections everywhere, including the music industry, and that helped him make the partnership happen. You have to remember, at the time, the Raptors were floundering as an on-court product, and they needed to keep fans engaged.

The move also appealed to Drake's support of the franchise and tugged at his hometown heartstrings. I don't know how much the move helped the team but it certainly didn't hurt. That was Leiweke's mentality while he was here. Take giant swings, and if you miss, you move on to the next idea. He was bold enough and saw that one small move could have a trickle-down effect on everything else in the organization.

During Leiweke's time here, the Raptors also landed an All-Star Game bid. Who can forget the press conference with Rob Ford and Drake announcing it? The mayor just looked completely out of his element, as if he'd been photoshopped into a picture he didn't belong in. The world of basketball was going to come to Toronto and here was the mayor looking like a whirlwind. I don't think they let Ford speak at all during the presser. He had to be there, because it was Toronto, but everyone was like, What is this guy doing here?

That was Leiweke. Go big or go home, and he was always going to go big.

"I want to bring the excitement into this building. I want a team that people are dying to come see. I want the tickets to be extremely hard to get," he said at his introductory news conference. "I want to bring that aggression, I want to bring that energy. Obviously, I want it to be a top team in the NBA, if not the top team."

Leiweke also talked openly about having the parade route mapped out for the Maple Leafs, which was another bold move, considering how long the city had been waiting for a Stanley Cup champion. Who would have thought he should have actually planned out a route for the Raptors instead? And, you know, sometimes bold is good; it was certainly new to Toronto and maybe too much. But what the hell, right? "I occasionally screwed it up by talking about stupid things that could happen if we won," he once said.

After just a year on the job, Leiweke announced in April 2014 that he would be leaving MLSE and that he would remain in the role for another year or until the organization named a successor. In October 2015, he formally stepped away from the job. Michael

Friisdahl was named as the new president and CEO of MLSE.

Even though he accomplished a lot during his short time in Toronto, Leiweke rubbed a lot of people at MLSE the wrong way. Some thought he was too loud and too brash. Others thought he loved to talk about his own accomplishments a little too much. He wasn't like any other leader they'd ever had. I'm not sure the board of directors really appreciated the way he went about his business. As it turns out, in retrospect, he helped lay the foundation for what would be a championship team, at least on the basketball side.

We always wondered how Leiweke and Tanenbaum would coexist long-term. Tanenbaum is a very reserved guy. He still doesn't attend games on Friday nights because he spends them with his family. He's much more private than how Leiweke was. I'm not sure anyone ever expected Leiweke to stay in Toronto long-term because that's just not how he operates. He likes to be challenged constantly, and people like him are always looking for what's next.

The board of directors was certainly happy to see him go. In a way, it was, "Hey, thanks for everything you've done here. Now we need a quieter guy to run the show." Leiweke's attitude reminds me a lot of Ujiri's. Both of them had a vision of how the Raptors were going to win in Toronto, and both had an unwavering belief that they were going to figure it out. In a way, Ujiri took the torch from Leiweke and became the voice of this organization.

The one constant through all the shuffling up top has been Tanenbaum. He's not a majority shareholder, but he's the guy who sits front row at all the games and he's been around basketball forever. He's supportive but never intrusive. Everyone in the organization calls him Mr. T. He has the respect of everyone around here. He could be a Mark Cuban or a James Dolan, but that's just not what

Tanenbaum is about. He spent years trying to land a basketball team in Toronto, and I'm sure he's more than happy to bask in the success of the team in his own private way.

I sat with Larry one day in 2014 in his office at his corporate headquarters in downtown Toronto, for one of the very few one-on-one interviews he's ever granted. It was obvious that he was passionate about his teams—the Raptors most of all—and passionate about his background role.

"The bright lights should never be on the owners," he told me that day. "They shouldn't be on Tim Leiweke or any CEO. The bright lights should rightfully be on Masai Ujiri, Brendan Shanahan, Tim Bezbatchenko [general manager of the city's MLS franchise]."

Tanenbaum and Ujiri have a close relationship. I think Tanenbaum truly does view him like a son, and there's a pride in watching how Ujiri has grown into who he is with this organization, how he was finally given this opportunity and he delivered on his promise of bringing a championship to Toronto.

Tanenbaum has a philanthropic nature to him that I think allows him to appreciate Ujiri outside of basketball as well. He appreciates how, through his foundation Giants of Africa and other charitable works, Ujiri has been able to make the organization bigger than just a basketball team.

Tanenbaum would love for the Raptors to be the first NBA team to play an exhibition game in Africa; he is intensely proud of the team's association with Right To Play, a group that advocates for inclusion in sports. He gives Ujiri every bit of support he needs for the president's Giants of Africa work. He loves the games and the wins and the sports; he loves the greater role his teams can play in the world just as much.

"Sports can really build things that are important to our society," he told me that day in 2014. "To have as a poster child the Toronto Raptors as our calling card can be a wonderful thing."

Ujiri is wired the same ways as guys like Leiweke. There's always a bigger challenge out there to pursue for someone of Ujiri's ambition. I don't envision him staying with the Raptors for the rest of his career, either. His next job might not even involve basketball. There's no telling. Ultimately, if Ujiri wants to stay, Tanenbaum and MLSE will pay him and give him anything he wants. I don't know if that will be enough. There will probably come a time when the organization will say goodbye to Ujiri. I don't think the two will ever part ways on bad terms. They've grown too much together and have shared goals, dreams, and responsibilities that are bigger than sports.

It's why watching Ujiri and Tanenbaum hoist the Larry O'Brien Trophy on the podium in Oakland felt so satisfying. Both of them have been through the hard times with this franchise. Tanenbaum lives and dies with every win and loss of this team. It must have felt so good to finally watch his team break through and win it all.

He pushed the process from the very start and stayed with it through every incarnation when he could easily have walked away after losing out on the original bidding process.

He didn't. It was nice and fitting to see him as the last man standing through it all.

16

THE WOMEN OF MLSE

When Masai Ujiri returned to the Toronto Raptors organization as general manager in 2013, he brought a new approach, a new way of thinking for the franchise. The Raptors were going to be a progressive organization, and that meant hiring the best people, regardless of their race or gender.

There had been other women in the organization before. For the first two decades, the most notable person was Doreen Doyle. She was like a mother hen to all the players. Working with the team for 20 years, Doyle assisted with players if they needed anything: a car, help for family members getting settled in the city. It was a huge responsibility, and the players and front office people loved her. She would get things done. All kinds of things.

In their infancy, the Raptors employed a scout, Walker D. Russell, a gregarious sort who was very much a basketball guy; his wardrobe was solely based on sweats and polo shirts and that was fine. But in year three, after Darrell Walker was fired as head coach mid-season, Walker D. had to come off the road to join the staff as an assistant coach. And Doreen worked her magic. In the span of about eight hours, she had not only found but also delivered a couple of new suits that Walker D. could wear on the bench—that was the kind of magic she could make happen.

There were others, of course, but not that many in the basketball side of the operation. Liana Bristol-Ward was an important part of the broadcast arm of the team. Lori Belanger was the first sideline reporter for television broadcast. Norma Wick moved from Vancouver to Toronto and became an early star on the team's cable TV network.

There weren't many other examples of women in prominent roles in the organization until Ujiri came along. It was a very conscious effort of his to increase opportunities for women. The Raptors wanted to get more women's voices in the organization, and it wasn't any kind of tokenism. They wanted to move away from the old-school approach that had become ingrained across all sports.

The people they hired would be from all walks of life. They didn't necessarily look to recycle the same executives, coaches, and trainers from around the league. You didn't need to have experience in the league or an intricate knowledge of the game or the sport of basketball. This was going to be a different approach.

The first woman Ujiri hired was Teresa Resch, now the team's vice president of basketball operations. Resch was the senior operations manager for Ultimate Hoops at Life Time Fitness when she took the Raptors job. She was a groundbreaker for the franchise. She's had her voice in various different things behind the scenes, and she's done very well.

Resch once told me she found the job to be tough at the start because she wasn't by nature an outgoing, talkative person. She needed to step outside of herself and be more assertive in offering her suggestions to other senior members of the organization. It didn't take long for her to realize that this was what the organization wanted. They didn't just hire her because she was a woman. They hired her because they valued her input.

"Masai says hire women, but then he backs it up," Resch once said. "He treats us the same as the guys and holds us accountable. He's not going to hold back. If I do something wrong, I'm going to hear about it. That's important. Women don't get special treatment, we get equal treatment. And nobody wants special treatment. You just want equal treatment, and he definitely does that."

One of the jobs Resch was tasked with was finding a new practice facility for the Raptors, helping to get it built, and overseeing the entire process. Fair or not, there was a lot of pressure on her to succeed. If Resch had failed at her job, it might have set back the movement of hiring more women, not just with the Raptors, but around the NBA and across all sports. I don't think it would have killed the idea of promoting women into important positions in front offices, but it might have slowed it down a little bit.

I still remember how proud she was at All-Star Weekend in 2016 in Toronto when the practice facility was finally unveiled to the public. In her six-plus years in the organization, Resch has done a tremendous job in any role she has been placed in, and I think she's paving the way for other women to follow her path, both inside and outside of the Raptors organization.

Shelby Weaver is another woman in the Raptors organization who has risen up the ranks. She started with the Raptors 905 minor league team and was brought along slowly, and now she's the manager of player development with the Raptors. Altogether, there are now 14 women in prominent positions in the organization, all since Ujiri's tenure.

Brittni Donaldson was initially brought on to help out with video and working in the back room away from the on-court action. She did such a wonderful job in her role that she was eventually promoted to the bench as an assistant coach. She had been a star player in high school and college in her native Iowa but had moved on to work in statistics and actuarial sciences when the Raptors came calling.

"I have great support here and everybody's bought in to the work I've put in," Donaldson says. "Our leadership here is really progressive and forward-thinking and open-minded. They don't see an exact formula to get to A to B. They just see someone who's capable and put them there."

Donaldson isn't the only one. In 2016, the Raptors hired Nicki Gross to be their player development coach for the Raptors 905. She worked under Jerry Stackhouse, who was the head coach of the game. Gross had joined the D-League several years back as an assistant video coordinator with the Bakersfield Jam, and then later was hired by the Iowa Energy in 2015 as an assistant coach.

At the time, Gross was the only female assistant coach in the D-League. But times have changed, especially in the NBA. Today, when a woman is hired to be an assistant coach, it doesn't lead the news cycle anymore. And that's a good thing. These things should normalize over time, and the NBA has always been the most progressive sports league in so many areas.

There will come a day when we will see a woman get hired as a head coach in the NBA. The Raptors are pretty settled at the head coaching position right now, especially coming off a championship, but I would put them at the top of the list of franchises who will lead the way in making that happen.

It is not just the coaching department. Women are prominent across the Raptors organization. Shannon Hosford is the chief marketing officer of the team. She was involved in the launch of the We the North campaign and was a huge driver in the 25th anniversary season celebrations that have been happening through-out the 2019–20 season. The Raptors also hired Sarah Chan to be their scouting manager in Africa. When Jim LaBumbard left to work for the NBA after the 2016 season, the Raptors hired *Toronto Star* sports editor Jennifer Quinn to run their PR department.

Having women in prominent roles is a corporate identity that is not lost on the players.

"It works for our team; it's refreshing to have women around and it's not weird; I don't really think of it as a thing at all," Fred VanVleet once told a Toronto newspaper. "This is my first NBA team, so it's all I've ever known in the league. We're a very diverse organization—men, women, players from many different countries with different points of view. It makes for a special place."

All of these hires showed Ujiri's approach when it came to bring-ing more women into the organization in vastly different roles. The organization wanted to cast a wide net in every hire they made and never limited themselves in considering people. It has set a very high standard, especially here in Toronto and across Canada, for other sports organizations to follow.

I would hope that other leagues, like the CFL and the NHL, are looking at what the Raptors are doing and seeing how much they've benefited by enabling so many women in important positions across the organization. The NBA is, in many ways, a model organization, and if it works here, hopefully it will encourage teams in other leagues to take on the same approach.

It's not just about celebrating how many women you have on the organizational chart. It's about expanding your talent pool. Don't hire women because they're women; hire women because they're good women and because they're good at their jobs.

That's the best message to send.

It's not just sports organizations looking to women, either. Many businesses can learn from what the Raptors are doing, too. These guys are successful, and part of the reason is their approach of bringing in fresh voices. If the Raptors are making a conscious effort in this regard, maybe other organizations can do it, too.

The message they're sending is not just to other organizations, it's to women who want to dream about one day working in sports, even if it's not in a playing capacity. They're showing younger women athletes, administrators, and coaches that you, too, can reach the top of your level, and if you're good at your job, the NBA will be paying attention, too.

"These are leading decision-makers in our business," Ujiri told me once. "There's nothing like showing [success] right in front of you, and I think Teresa, Shannon, and Sarah really proved that, the 14 women who work for the Raptors proved that. They were not hired because we wanted to hire women, they were hired because they're the best at what they do."

Ujiri had strong women around him all his life. His biggest influence was his mom, Paula Grace, a doctor who was supportive of Ujiri but who also always pushed him. Grace let her son know that since he wasn't going to be good enough to be an NBA player, he had to go out in the world and figure out what he was going to be.

"She said, 'You are going out into the world now, go out and do your best, go out and conquer,'" Ujiri said. "I believe in every woman because of that. She inspired me to challenge, to compete, and not to be afraid, and while you do this, always care for people."

It was his wife, Ramatu, who was the driving force in pushing Ujiri to leave the Raptors organization in his first go-round in order to take the general manager job with the Denver Nuggets. It was time for Ujiri to make a bold step in his career and try for something more.

The advice and support Ujiri has received through the years from women in his life has resonated with him, and he's carried that to the organization he works for. It's now ingrained within the Raptors franchise. They're going to look everywhere to find the best people, and in places where other teams might not even think about looking.

The more diverse backgrounds and diverse voices you have in a room, the better you're ultimately going to be. If we've learned anything from the Raptors, it's that when you have these different voices, it lets you tackle problems from different angles.

"And by the way," Ujiri said, "if anyone wants to question it—we won a championship."

17

PLAYER DEVELOPMENT

If there's one advantage the Toronto Raptors have over the rest of the NBA, it is their player development. When we look back at this present era of Raptors basketball, how this franchise has been able to consistently bring unproven young players into their system and mould them into rotation guys and even superstars has been remarkable.

In their first two decades of existence, the Raptors weren't exactly known as the most forward-thinking franchise in the league. In their defence, neither was the rest of the NBA. So much of building a roster depended on convincing star players to sign with them in free agency, winning trades, and drafting well. Second-round draft picks were fliers, often unknown European teenagers whose development was left to their club teams; the idea that club teams would have hands-on experience in developing talent was basically unheard of.

The Raptors didn't use second-round picks as afterthoughts—that would diminish the work of scouts they employed and no one wants to take away from their legitimate hard work—but they knew that if they hit on one good player, it would be little more than a fluke.

Look at some of the names and backgrounds: Tyson Wheeler of Rhode Island, DeeAndre Hulett of the College of the Sequoias, Remon Van de Hare of the Netherlands, Albert Miralles of Spain, Edin Bavčić of Bosnia. These guys aren't household names even in their own households, and they played as many NBA games combined as I have.

As the game became more global each year and with the expanded talent pool—and the fact that only 60 players are selected in the draft each year—there was an opportunity for teams to exploit a market inefficiency: if you could put together a competent plan for developing young players, you could do just as well as teams who were tanking and drafting in the lottery every year.

In a way, you could have the best of both worlds: advance a winning program and make the playoffs every season while simultaneously developing a young core.

It's exactly what the Raptors have done.

All the credit goes to Masai Ujiri and everyone in the organization who has worked tirelessly on the scouting and player development side. And it might have taken a failed experiment for them to realize how important it was to create an advantage for themselves.

In 2014, the Raptors drafted a kid from Brazil named Bruno Caboclo with the 20th overall pick. On draft night, it surprised every single scout and media expert. Nobody had heard of this kid, and if they did, they didn't think Caboclo was going to have his name called in the first round. ESPN's Fran Fraschilla famously said he was two years away from being two years away.

For a kid like this to come to a winning program like the Raptors was difficult. He was a long-term development project, and it didn't help that he wasn't going to get a chance to play much at the NBA level. Add in the fact that you have to adjust to living in a new country, and it's a lot to ask a teenager to shoulder.

The Raptors did the sensible thing and sent him on assignments in the D-League. The problem was, Toronto didn't have their own league affiliate. So Caboclo was being shipped off to play with the Fort Wayne Mad Ants, a team that wasn't fully affiliated with the Raptors organization and didn't have the developmental interest of Caboclo as their priority. No one there gave a rat's ass about him. And why would they? The ties to the Raptors were non-existent, and the Mad Ants owners needed to field a team that won games, not one that taught young players organizational goals.

So Caboclo would get limited minutes in the G-League, as the D-League came to be known, but there wasn't a coaching staff from the Raptors organization to steer and guide him, to make sure he was put in a position to grow. It stagnated his progress. When he was with the Raptors, they—like every other NBA team—would rarely have practice time during the regular season. There was simply no room for him to develop those first few seasons here.

Now, consider if they had let him play professionally in Europe after the draft and put him somewhere in an environment where he could learn to be a pro and develop his skills. In that hypothetical scenario, the Raptors could have sent someone from their organization to check in on him regularly and worked with a pro team overseas on a developmental program for Caboclo. You stash him there a few years, give him a regular routine and consistent minutes as a pro player, and see what you've got.

Caboclo was nicknamed the Brazilian Kevin Durant. When you looked at his body, it was comparable to Durant's. He has these long, long arms. He was quick and with a wide wingspan, but being a pro is so much more than just learning about dribbling and shooting. And this kid never had that.

The Raptors were on their way to acquiring their own G-League team anyway, but I think seeing what unfolded with Caboclo might have sped up the process. Draft capital is important to every team. Even turning one first-rounder drafting in the 20s into a rotation player can be the difference between a contending team and one that misses the playoffs.

The Raptors didn't want to take chances anymore with their young guys, so the team announced their own G-League team, the Raptors 905, who would play out of Mississauga, less than an hour's drive away from Scotiabank Arena, starting with the 2015–16 season.

G-League teams don't make money, but their value is in the development, which, to a franchise like the Raptors, is priceless. Any NBA franchise can absorb the financial losses. Bobby Webster, the team's current general manager, once told me the organization loses about a million dollars running the 905 every financial year.

The return on investment, though, is the long list of unproven prospects who turned into core pieces on a championship team. The list includes Pascal Siakam, who won the G-League finals MVP and honed his craft there before eventually becoming an all-star player and a crucial piece to the 2018–19 team that won the championship.

There was Fred VanVleet, the undrafted guard out of Wichita State who also developed his game with the Raptors 905 and who eventually became not only an integral part of the Raptors' success on the court but a leader in the locker room as well. It's pretty neat to think about VanVleet's journey, from undrafted kid to earning an NBA finals MVP vote from Hubie Brown.

That those two—a late first-round draft pick who honed his

Isiah Thomas bursting through the team's logo at the 1994 news conference to announce his appointment as the team's first president and a minority owner was a landmark occasion. It gave the first real face to the expansion team and bestowed on it a measure of legitimacy.

Some fans at what was then known as the SkyDome booed when Damon Stoudamire was announced as the first college draft pick in Raptors history. Those boos didn't last long— Mighty Mouse won over the fans with his play and was the 1995–96 NBA rookie of the year.

It's been a long journey; I've been covering the Raptors since the day the franchise was awarded in 1994. Being there every step of the way meant witnessing the ascension of basketball in Canada; the sport has gone from an afterthought to a game that truly grips the nation coast to coast, as the euphoria of the 2019 NBA championship showed.

A couple of tickets to opening night in 1995 were admission to an event no Toronto fan had ever experienced. There were blips—when thunderstick noisemakers were handed out to fans under the wrong basket—but that night had the atmosphere of a monumental occasion and the beginning of a new era in Toronto.

John Salley, taken by the Raptors in the expansion draft, was one of the few recognizable names among the veterans who suited up for that first game. His tenure lasted less than a season—he was released before the season was even halfway done—but he celebrated with teammates after the opening night win.

Brendan Malone, the first coach in franchise history, often found himself in the throes of a dilemma. He was an excellent teacher but he wanted to win more than anything, which often placed him at odds with general manager Isiah Thomas, who was more interested in player development.

© Jonathan Daniel / Stringer, Allsport, Getty Images

Much of the Raptors marketing in the early years of the franchise's existence was built around coaxing fans to come watch the league superstars. And no star shone more brightly than Michael Jordan, who squared off against Toronto's own budding star Damon Stoudamire, in 1995.

© Stephen Dunn / Staff, Getty Images

Darrell Walker, who succeeded Brendan Malone and became the second head coach, was in an unenviable position. He was not prepared to be a head coach when he got the job and was saddled with a roster lacking NBA talent. He lasted about a year and half before he was replaced by Butch Carter in 1998.

The watershed moment in the rise of the Raptors came in 1998 when Vince Carter was obtained in a pre-arranged draft night trade with the Golden State Warriors. It was, as it was called, Vinsanity around the team, thanks to Carter's high-flying dunks that brought validation to the young franchise.

Vince Carter's impact was immediate. Playing a shortened, 50-game season due to lockout, he became the second Raptor to win the league's Rookie of the Year award, joining Damon Stoudamire. It established him as one of the most promising young players in the league.

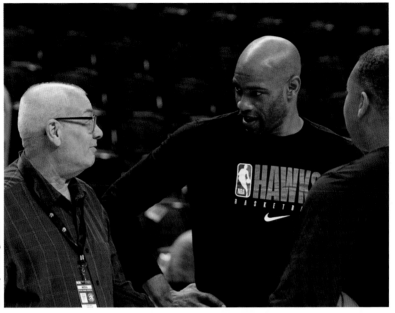

Twenty-two years after he became a Raptor, Vince Carter paid his final visit as a player to Toronto as a member of the Atlanta Hawks in the 2019–20 season. He ended up playing more seasons than any player in league history and retired at peace with the franchise that traded him and fans who had once vilified him.

Charles Oakley was one of the most significant players during the late 1990s and early 2000s, a veteran whose presence helped teach young players like Vince Carter to be professionals. He was also one of the most quotable players of all time: "It's like bringing eggs to a barbecue" and "Just because there's glass on the highway doesn't mean there was an accident" were two of his best lines.

Percy Miller—Master P, as he was known—was a globally famous rapper when the Raptors invited him to training camp in 1999. Some saw it as a publicity stunt, a desperation move by the franchise to court some kind of legitimacy with young fans. Master P was cut before camp was over, for entirely legitimate basketball reasons.

The most enduring symbol of the franchise from day one has been The Raptor, the mascot who has an incalculable connection with the team's fans. The antics were, some nights, the most entertaining aspect of the game; keeping fans engaged when their team is losing is no easy task.

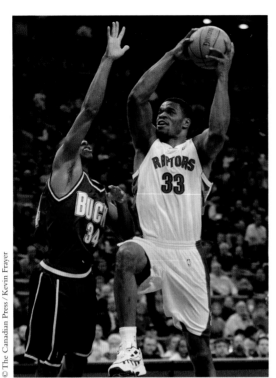

Antonio Davis was, at times, unhappy to be in Toronto; he complained about the education his children were getting and other aspects of playing in a foreign land. He came to accept his locale and his play on the court was exemplary—he put the team on his back during a late-season surge to the 2001–02 playoffs.

When you draw up the list of underrated Raptors, Doug Christie should be right at the top. He played on some bad teams but was an outstanding player, maybe the best individual defender the team ever had. He clashed with then-coach Butch Carter at the end of his Toronto tenure, but that does not take away from his overall on-court contribution.

The Vancouver Grizzlies and Raptors came into the NBA at the same time but only one franchise survived. Ownership and business issues sent the Grizzlies packing for Memphis after the 2000–01 season, ending what had been a budding Canadian rivalry.

Hall of Famer Lenny Wilkens was not the hardest working coach in franchise history but he did guide the Raptors to their first playoff series win in 2001. His development of and faith in young guard Alvin Williams was one of Wilkens's major contributions to the franchise.

Early in their existence, the Raptors tried to capitalize on cross-sports marketing in hockey-mad Toronto. Hockey stars such as Leafs goaltender Ed Belfour, along with recording artists and actors, were all regular spectators at games. They were also often urged to take part in on-court antics during timeouts and breaks in play.

Canadian basketball icon Jay Triano, shown here with José Calderón, became the first Canadian head coach in NBA history when he took over from Sam Mitchell in 2008. Triano was the standard-bearer for a growing number of Canadian coaches who are now working at the highest level of the sport.

DeMar DeRozan, chosen ninth overall in the NBA draft, arrived as a relative unknown in 2009. The quiet teenager from Compton, California, was in the starting lineup his rookie season, forging a major role on a struggling roster.

DeRozan became one of the most popular players to ever wear a Raptors uniform during his nine seasons in Toronto, and getting to know him as a person as well as a player was a great part of covering his career. Catching up with him during the 2019–20 season in the hallways of Scotiabank Arena was a nice, private moment.

Kyle Lowry is something of an artist on the NBA hardwood but he's also willing to try to navigate the NHL ice at times. Players on the Raptors and NHL Maple Leafs have always had an interest not only in the fortunes of their corporate cousins but an appreciation for how hard the other's jobs are.

Superfan Nav Bhatia has been a staple around the team, as recognizable as any of the players thanks to his courtside and demonstrative nature. He can get as excited about a big basket or win as anyone, as witnessed in this joint celebration with Kyle Lowry.

Dwane Casey arrived in Toronto in 2011 and immediately set the franchise on course to the 2019 championship. The long-time NBA assistant coach preached teamwork, defence, and consistency of effort as he helped grow the team into a championship contender over his seven seasons at the helm.

Dwane Casey, here with myself and Mike Ganter of the *Toronto Sun*, accepting an award from the Professional Basketball Writers Association in 2016, is one of the most genuinely good people to ever work for the Raptors. He may not have been around for the championship season, but his impact was felt all throughout it.

When the Raptors made Drake the team's Global Ambassador in 2014, no one really knew what that meant. But the Toronto native and lifelong Raptors fan has been a staple at games, as enthusiastic as any fan in the building, and helped create a buzz about the team among his fans worldwide.

He was a supernova of sorts. No one knew what Kawhi Leonard would bring when he was obtained in a 2018 trade for the beloved DeMar DeRozan but he had an incredible season culminating in an NBA championship. He may not have been all fuzzy and warm with fans or media but there was no denying his abundant talent.

The night of June 13, 2019, in Oakland was a magical one indeed. By winning the first NBA championship in franchise history, the Raptors capped off an incredible season and set off a raucous celebration that spanned across Canada. The group placed itself firmly in the Canadian sports history record books.

Kyle Lowry calls it "the golden ball" and it is what every NBA player dreams of touching one day. For beat reporters who were part of the journey, the chance to hang out up close and personal with the Larry O'Brien Trophy is a pretty special feeling, as well.

A crowd estimated at two million people, the largest parade gathering in Canadian sports history, spent an exhausting, celebratory day with the Raptors in June, 2019, rejoicing in the team's NBA championship. It was an outpouring of love that had never before been experienced.

The architect of it all, Raptors president Masai Ujiri. Not only is he one of the most astute judges of talent in the game, but his ability to inspire and lead people in any number of ways makes him special. Ujiri's worldview and sense of social responsibility eclipse his sports acumen.

The singing of "O Canada" before Game 1 of the 2019 NBA Finals was one of the most emotional moments of my career. It was the culmination of a slog that lasted more than two decades and I cannot imagine recapturing the same monumental feeling I had that evening.

skills leading the 905 to a G-League title as the finals MVP and an undrafted guard who spent days and days practising with the Raptors in the late morning and playing for the 905 that night— were so instrumental in a championship run is amazing, and a testament to the powers of institutional player development.

Oh, each had skill, there's no denying that, but the chance to learn and expand that skill set was only possible because of the existence of the minor league team.

The list of players goes on, and I think the Raptors are just getting started. Chris Boucher is another former G-League mainstay who has since cracked the rotation with the big club. Last year, the Raptors signed undrafted guard Terence Davis during summer league, and it seems like now the player development curve has been shortened. All of us expected Davis to spend the majority of his rookie season with the Raptors 905. Instead, he quickly developed into a rotation player with the defending champions.

Davis is a prime example of how the track record of Toronto's recent success in player development has made it an appealing destination for younger players around the league. Davis certainly had other options. He played for the Denver Nuggets in the Las Vegas Summer League and could have waited out different teams to see what kinds of offers he would have received.

But he chose the Raptors because Davis saw what they've been able to do with players like Siakam and VanVleet. It's a bit of a self-fulfilling prophecy. You see the success of others and you want to come and follow that same path, too. The franchise has a well-earned reputation around the league, and it's a valuable advantage especially when you're not a premier free agent destination for most star players.

The NBA is all about finding guys that other teams aren't looking at. The draft is a crapshoot. Free agency can be so expensive that it hampers your financial flexibility. Finding and developing players is often the difference between a good and bad team. And as long as the Raptors 905 have been around, the Raptors have been a successful team. I don't see any reason to think that's going to change.

Having a G-League team isn't just about the players either. The Raptors are also using their minor league organization as a way to groom coaches, trainers, public relations staff, and those in all other positions. There's a consistent message about development across the entire organization. Nick Nurse, who coached for many years in the D-League, says it all the time: to become a head coach you have to learn to be one. The 905 has provided a place for coaches to get that experience. I don't know if current 905 coach Jama Mahlalela will ever become an NBA head coach, but his experience there will certainly help him. His predecessor was Jesse Mermuys, and he did such a fantastic job that it helped him land an assistant coaching job in Los Angeles and later in Sacramento.

"It helps us develop players, I think that's number one, but we're also going to use this as an experiment," Masai Ujiri once said in the run-up to the first 905 game. "We're going to use this as a guinea pig in some ways, whether it's modelling our front office or modelling what the coaches are doing, instructing, teaching. We're going to try everything."

He was right. Of all the things they've done over the past decade, getting a G-League team of their own in Mississauga was the best one this organization did. The players get consistent teaching principles, and the coaches, at the big-league level and at the G-League, work in unison. There's a consistent program in place for skill development and style of play. It is the perfect incubator system.

The close proximity of the two clubs is a huge advantage, too. You can practice with the Raptors in the morning and play that evening with the 905. If a player isn't getting enough minutes with the big club, he can request an assignment in Mississauga to get some run in and stay sharp. Other times, it is a matter of convenience. If the Raptors need an injury replacement, they can call a player up and have him at the arena in no time.

The stuff you learn there, as a player or as a coach, just helps you get better and gives you a better chance at the next level. Player development is now a popular thing around the league. Every sports league is a copycat league. If one team finds success with something, everyone else will rush to see if they can follow the same blueprint. I believe we're just a few years away from all 30 NBA teams having their own minor league affiliate.

The NBA is more and more about developing your own guys, especially because there are only a handful of superstars who can truly change the fortune of a franchise by themselves. LeBron James. Kevin Durant. Stephen Curry. Kawhi Leonard. The list gets short pretty quick. In this day and age, you have to find guys on your own and tap into their potential.

To this day, I still believe Caboclo would have been a useful player for the Raptors if they'd had a program for him in place. If the Raptors 905 were here when he was a rookie, maybe he'd still be part of this team. He might have to settle for being the cautionary tale that helped kickstart Toronto's quest to become the best team in the NBA at player development.

I think back to the first two decades of this franchise and how not having this system in place hurt the team. In a way, it didn't hurt anyone because few franchises had this type of set-up. Overall, I think the NBA missed the boat. They thought they had the perfect development system in the NCAA, but that turned out to be false.

There's a lot of talent in Division I college basketball, but some of these kids come to the NBA and haven't learned how to be grown adults, or how to properly dribble, shoot, or play. Without a minor league affiliate, a lot of these kids are lost the moment they sign their first NBA contract, and within a few years, they're out of the league. With this new system in place, every team is hopeful they can develop a similar pipeline as the Raptors have.

So, what makes the Raptors better than most other teams in the NBA in this regard? The organization surely won't share all of their trade secrets publicly. But there's a sense that they are able to start their messaging during the summer. When players are having individual workouts in July and August, they send coaches around the country and around the world to work with these guys. There's a consistency to it, and the coaches really hone in on areas they want players to improve on.

I'm not sure if every NBA team has a coaching staff and people within the organization who are willing to make that kind of commitment to their players. It's a year-round process. And don't forget, we talk so much about the development of these young, unproven guys, but even established NBA players like DeMar DeRozan and Serge Ibaka have watched their games grow by working with this organization.

So, what's next? The Raptors are continuing to pour resources into finding the best players available around the world. Through Giants of Africa, Ujiri has plenty of connections and people on the ground, keeping close tabs on the next generation of basketball players who will come from that continent. Ujiri is a well-respected beacon for basketball over there, and as a result, the Raptors have a different level of respect there than all other NBA teams.

I would not be surprised at all if the Raptors continue to unearth guys who are undrafted or select players you've never heard of and turn them into rotation players on a playoff team. Players around the world know about the Raptors, and their reputation gets them in the door for a chance to sign all these guys.

This is just the beginning.

18

TRAINING FACILITIES

Nothing traces the evolution of the Raptors over a quarter of a century more than walking through the franchise's training facilities, from the first one that you could barely find with a search warrant to the current home named after the company headed by the global ambassador, Drake, and emblazoned with its logo. From Glendon College to the training facility in the home arena to the opulent OVO Athletic Centre: each had its charms and you can measure the franchise's growth by examining where the team has lived all these years.

You turned east off Toronto's Yonge Street onto a tiny road that looked like it led to nowhere. Down a hill, around a corner, into a parking lot amid a stand of trees you went. Out of the car parked in the elements—no private entrance into a heated indoor parking facility for the first Raptors, no sir, not at all—for a short walk over a tiny bridge across a small creek and into a small building tucked away at the base of a hill. Up a flight of stairs and there was the gym, a tiny multi-purpose gym with one basketball court and a couple of rows of retractable stands that were standard in every high school gym in the province at the time.

The locker room was small, there were no offices or meeting spaces or dining areas, and at about one o'clock every practice day the session had to end because the girls volleyball team was coming in, come hell or high water, and if the NBA team had to end its day before the coaches wanted it to end, well, tough noogies for them. It was a monstrous pain in the ass for the reporters but we were so new to the business that we didn't really know it at the time.

There was no chance at any post-practice idle chit-chat and interviews were conducted hurriedly on the court before volleyball or in a hallway outside the locker room, but we made do because we didn't have anything to compare it to. And, besides, there might be eight of us on a busy day, not like today, when there are routinely two dozen or more people holding tape recorders or notebooks or cameras covering even the most mundane of practices.

We and they were guests and tenants and not owners, and the volleyball practice or intramural games had to proceed apace.

Yes, the times have indeed changed.

It's not that the Proctor Field House on the campus of Glendon College deep in the heart of urban Toronto was a bad facility, of course. It was a court and the players could get some work in each day, and since there weren't a plethora of possibilities available to the Raptors, it had to do and it served its purpose. Practising where they played was out of the question because of the SkyDome baseball games and concerts and car shows and what have you that took priority.

"It was a miracle that it worked out because there wasn't any real place," recalls Glen Grunwald, at that time the number two executive to team president Isiah Thomas and the point man for all things operational. "I had been all over the place. I had spoken to Ken Olynyk at the University of Toronto and he was trying to make it work there, but there was no real schedule that made sense because obviously the university and the students were the first priority. And then I think I was talking to him about what other places are there and he said, 'Well, you know, Glendon College has a facility.' I went over there and there was a super nice guy who ran the facility and he was really accommodating."

It wasn't perfect but it was home. Sort of.

"There were limitations but it was good enough," Grunwald said. "It could have been a lot worse. We had looked everywhere. We had looked at an armoury over by the downtown area, we had talked about that. We were up at Downsview Park, there was an old gymnasium there that was sort of closed down. But I think Glendon College did turn out to be reasonably acceptable. Very nice folks there that worked with us and it looked pretty good."

And back then, practices were so open to the media that nothing went unnoticed, like the last day the eminently forgettable Benoit Benjamin spent with the Raptors.

Near the end of that practice—and reporters were about three metres away from court because there was nowhere else to watch from—coach Darrell Walker was rather vociferously urging the somewhat lackadaisical Benjamin to work harder, run faster during some final sprints.

Benjamin was having none of it, totally resentful of being asked to work harder at his job, and he finally let Walker have it, rattling off a stream of invectives and creative curses—"Eff you, you bitch-faced MFer" was how it's recalled. Walker, perhaps mindful of the presence of the media, somehow managed to hold his temper and not get into a fist fight, but it was less than an hour after the outburst that the team announced Benjamin had been waived and cut, his Raptors career ending on the court at the tiny practice facility that was the team's first home. Of all the days we stood in that gym, pushed up against a couple of rows of bleachers watching a bad team going about its business, that might have been the most memorable moment of them all.

There was a "home" in between Glendon College and the current facility, and much like the evolution of the franchise itself over a quarter of a century, it was something of a middle ground between the infancy of the Raptors and their arrival as a true, consistent power in the NBA.

Stuck off the third-floor concourse of the Scotiabank Arena, barely noticeable to the hundreds of thousands of fans who walk by it over the course of a season, is the team's first privately owned and run practice facility.

It is tiny—one court and a small weight room three storeys above the team's locker room—and accessible only by walking among the people if there's some event being held in the arena. It was sufficient for a few years but hardly anything to brag about.

It opened in 1999 along with what was then known as the Air Canada Centre and served its purpose for almost 17 years. And it was called a lot of things depending on the sponsorship deals of the day—the Flight Deck, the Nike Practice Facility, now just the Practice Facility if you ever notice the signage outside the arena on its facade at the west end—but it should be permanently named the John Wallace Gym because the long-forgotten Raptor was instrumental in its coming into existence.

In a three-team trade in 1997 between the Raptors, the New York Knicks, and the Portland Trail Blazers, which centred around Wallace to Toronto and Chris Dudley from Portland to New York, the Raptors coaxed an additional $1 million out of the deal, which went to adding the practice facility to the plans for what became the Air Canada Centre.

"We got a million dollars from the Knicks for taking John Wallace, and it wasn't directly correlated to getting the money for the practice facility, but it helped a lot," Grunwald recalled. "As they were doing cost engineering or value engineering, the practice facility was at risk, let's say. I think the million dollars we got from John Wallace helped us get the practice facility."

It did exist through some memorable times, though.

It's where Vince Carter practiced the moves that he used to win the 2001 NBA Slam Dunk Contest in one of the most memorable performances ever, it's where the team worked through its first five playoff appearances, and its intimacy created some special moments between reporters, players, and coaches. We didn't get to see Vince Carter practice his memorable dunk-contest dunks because he did that at night, but we did catch a glimpse of DeMar DeRozan working his. Sam Mitchell used to hold court every single day, sometimes for hours on end, talking life or strategy or whatever was on his mind. He once held a bit of a tutorial for us on the concept of "spacing" and was moving some of us around like chess pieces to explain in detail how one giant step could create enough "space" for a player to get a shot off. It was nice and informal in a nice and informal setting.

It was crowded, though. The sidelines and baselines were right up against the wall, and the danger of a player falling back into us while he worked on his show and we stood and waited was real. In the playoffs, the crowds became simply too much, and they ended up moving us out onto the concourse to conduct our interviews.

There was just one entrance to the gym—through a small door and around a corner—and everyone congregated just inside the doorway, so there was nowhere for players to hide.

Charles Oakley had to be physically restrained by team public relations officials more than a few times—jokingly, of course—when he wanted to leave before fulfilling his media obligations.

Antonio Davis once left screaming and hollering at Dave Perkins of the *Toronto Star* for something Perkins had written that struck a nerve with him. Dave had written something about Antonio's wife, Kendra, who never had an opinion she didn't want to share, and Davis wanted to make sure Perkins knew he felt families were off-limits.

And during the final days of Butch Carter's reign as the team's head coach, a handful of players—Doug Christie and Dee Brown chief among them—held court in the doorway absolutely ripping the coach. Carter had sued Marcus Camby, and that was a distraction the players hated. He had told the players they couldn't wear headbands, so they immediately started wearing them and took great glee in telling us. It was an "Eff you" moment we all wrote about.

The team may have thought that one access point was troublesome and a design flaw but reporters loved it because there was no way the players could sneak away without answering questions.

Those days are gone now, sadly. Now the OVO Athletic Centre—the Raptors' training facility on the western edge of the Canadian National Exhibition grounds near downtown Toronto—is antiseptic and opulent and too private for the media's needs, but perfect for the players, coaches, and management.

Down one of its hallways is something billed as a "technologically advanced cognitive operations centre." It is a fancy name for a war room, with a curved wall of interactive screens and a tabletop with more screens where every imaginable bit of information and video on hundreds and hundreds of NBA players and wannabes is just a swipe of the fingers away. It's state of the art and perfectly fitting for a $28 million, 68,000-square-foot facility that has every possible amenity available to players, coaches, and front office personnel.

It opened to much fanfare on the weekend Toronto hosted the NBA All-Star Game in February 2016 and was the culmination of nearly a decade of planning and hoping and cajoling and spending on a place the team could really call home.

When I first toured it, I was agog. So many first-class facilities, so much privacy, so much comfort; it ran counter to everything I'd ever seen in a Raptors practice facility. I knew the players would love it because it kept them in the style they had become accustomed to—new, high-end facilities from top to bottom—and it gave them a place that was truly theirs. No sharing it with a volleyball team, no sharing an arena gym with whatever was going on in the building. This was a home.

Of course, reasonably acceptable does not count these days, when opulence is the order of the day. It's why one of the very first tasks Masai Ujiri was given when Bryan Colangelo first hired him in 2007 was to figure out a new home for the team, and it took nearly a decade for it to come to fruition.

What a place it is.

Two full courts, a workout and weight-room area that would shame most private health clubs, a 30-or-so-seat theatre for watching video before and after practices, offices for everyone who is anyone in the organization, and privacy above all.

There's underground parking for the players, a private entrance and exit at the southern end of the building and as far away from the prying eyes of the media as possible, and a private chef with a restaurant-quality kitchen to work in.

There's a barbershop, for God's sake, and an underwater treadmill that's part of the state-of-the-art medical facilities, and an outdoor patio and barbecue area that runs the length of the building and affords the players a view of boats sailing on Lake Ontario if they want—if they want to leave the comfort of the locker room with its individual television monitors above each locker.

Yeah, it's a nice home that mere mortals can only dream of, but home in the NBA isn't like home anywhere else.

"It's when you don't have it that it's a question," Ujiri said during a tour when the building first opened. "When you don't have it, when [players] come to visit, the question comes up: Where's your practice facility? Now no one is going to ask the question, they'll know 'You know what, that's one thing they have, and it's great, it's new.' It's a huge advantage."

As Grunwald said: "It's unbelievable what happens now but good for everyone. It's an arms race now in the practice facility."

But—and maybe this is just an old head thinking about better, simpler times—there seemed to be more stories, more memories that came with the older, smaller, more intimate homes. Sure, it's nice and necessary to adapt with the times and coddle players so the reputation of the franchise around the league doesn't take a hit, but the stories were better.

Still, what self-serving sports organization doesn't need a war room that looks like it comes from some futuristic movie or some tech-savvy TV show?

"There's a lot of thinking that goes on in there, a lot of debating, a lot of questioning, a lot of research, and when you do all these things, you want all the right information in front of you all at once," Ujiri crowed when he was first showing it off. "When we have these digital machines and screens on our table, it puts all this information right in front of us to make important decisions in our organization."

Just another part of the evolution of the Raptors.

19

KYLE LOWRY

The championship banner that hangs from the rafters in the home arena of the Raptors will forever be a testament to the 2019 NBA title winners and to Kyle Lowry, who was front and centre as it was unfurled to thunderous applause on a late October night that year. He was the de facto master of ceremonies for the unfurling and will be forever remembered for the integral part he played in the magical ride and his constant presence as the franchise grew from virtually nothing into something very special.

"On behalf of my teammates, the organization . . . we want to thank all you fans and the great city of Toronto and the country of Canada. We wouldn't have been able to do that without you guys," was how he put it, and after gathering all his teammates around him, the countdown from five echoed through the arena with Lowry leading the chorus.

"We got this special thing up there we about to unveil . . . we going to do this together."

The same fans had chanted, "Lowry, Lowry, Lowry" after the

team clinched the Eastern Conference championship—a moment that gave me goosebumps as I watched it—and this was a fitting role for the most important player to play for the team.

Goosebumps, I tell you. I had them that ring-ceremony night like I'd never had them at a Raptors game before.

Lowry will always be known as one of the toughest and the very best to ever put on a Raptors uniform. His place in franchise lore is cemented.

But his rise to prominence, his emergence as the face of the franchise, did not come easily and is one of the great tales of players to have come and gone over the years.

The transformation of Lowry has been complete and shocking and wonderful for those in and around the organization who got to know him and for fans who wanted to embrace him and finally did.

Lowry's first training camp as a member of the Raptors was in 2012 in Halifax, and no one knew what to expect. About two months earlier, Bryan Colangelo had made what turned out to be the best trade of his time as the team's president and general manager, moving a bit piece Gary Forbes and a draft pick to the Houston Rockets for Lowry, who at that point was an unproven 26-year-old kid who had really done little to make himself a presence in the league.

The summertime transaction was basically an afterthought. At that time, Forbes, a guy who no one thought would ever amount to much, and the future draft pick were no more than throw-ins in exchange for Lowry, who was joining his third team in six seasons after so-so stints in Memphis and Houston.

The Raptors already had a proven point guard and a fan favourite in José Calderón, and Calderón had run off everyone who tried to take his job. Lowry, small and a bit paunchy and hardly a burgeoning talent, was surely going to go the way of Jarrett Jack and Jerryd Bayless and TJ Ford and Roko Ukić, all pretenders to Calderón's throne. Lowry wasn't going to be any different, I suspected. His reputation, as I had heard from friends who covered him in Memphis and in Houston, was that he was a prickly sort who was never in great shape and always in conflict with his head coaches.

Hell, the Raptors were so worried about his attitude they brought back Alvin Williams as an assistant coach and unofficial Kyle-minder because Williams knew Lowry. They both grew up in Philadelphia and went to Villanova there. Lowry was a hard-ass, I'd been told, and Calderón, who had endeared himself to coaches, teammates, and the media because he was personable, chatty, friendly, and very good at basketball, didn't have a thing to worry about, I figured.

"This is my eighth season. I always have to compete with another guy, it doesn't matter," Calderón said back at the time. "I look at it like always: you have to compete to be starting or if not, at the end of the day, the coach is the one who gives you more or less minutes. I don't know what Kyle thinks about it . . . at the end of the day, we have to co-exist if you want to win games."

No one knew what Lowry thought of it because—and he'll be the first to admit this and often has—when he first joined the Raptors, he was a bit of a dick.

That first training camp in Halifax, he was injured, and that gave him every excuse to blow off any media obligations, and when he did deign to talk, it'd be one-word answers, hardly engaging con-versations. He'd sit against the wall of the gym at the Canada Games Centre, surrounded by reporters and cameramen, and be a surly, non-communicative, unwilling participant in media sessions. If we needed him to comment for a story, he'd answer questions briefly if at all. He didn't want to know us and didn't want us to know him, and frankly, we disliked him intensely right off the bat.

A couple of days he simply said, "I ain't talking" and he didn't. Team officials disliked him because he took no responsibility for the media obligations he had to do. We'd complain and they'd shake their heads, tell us they couldn't get through to him, and if they ever did, it was going to take time. Reporters wanted nothing to do with him because it wasn't worth the effort. Besides, he'd be gone soon and what would it matter?

"Oh, I was a dick," he admitted in early 2020. "I still am a dick. It's okay. It don't matter."

Lowry's "I don't give a crap" level truly is off the charts. He plays for his teammates and his friends and his coaches and himself, and that's always been the case. He'll stand and fulfill his post-game media obligations on nights when he's been by far the best player on the court, dropping 30 points and 15 rebounds on some poor, overmatched opponent, and he'll steer the conversation to some teammate and what he did rather than take all the accolades himself.

His play became exemplary. Whenever a big play was needed—a charge taken for an offensive foul, a big three-pointer needed to seal a win, a pass or a defensive stop—he'd do it.

"I've never seen anyone play harder than this guy," Nick Nurse once said. "Ever. And that to me is like the ultimate compliment. I've never seen anybody play harder than this guy. And there's times in those film sessions, where I just, I can't believe it."

And then the coach gave a specific example from the 2019 NBA finals.

"There was one play where we were showing the other day, we went triangle-and-two in Game 5, and he ran out and challenged a shot over on the left wing; it bounced and went; he was pressuring Iguodala; the passer Curry came off here and he ran over and challenged it, and the ball bounced on the rim and went flying that way, and he was the one, he came skipping through about three guys and grabbed that rebound. I mean, I'm showing that to the team and telling them, 'Can anybody else? What if we all start doing that, just a little bit?'"

But Lowry's also got a passive-aggressive streak. He always knows that you know how good he is and how valuable he has been, yet he'll never say it out loud. In fact, he'll go to great lengths to remind the world that he doesn't really care.

"People got their own opinions," he said at one point during Toronto's championship run of 2019. "They can say what they want to say. They always have. I hear them, I listen, but they don't affect my life. Everyone has their own opinions. And I go out there and I do my job to the best of my abilities. And the people that know, my teammates, the organization, they know what I bring to the table, and they appreciate what I do and what I've done. And if I score zero points, people blah, blah, blah, I do this, I don't score. I understand what people say, I hear them. But if we win a game and we win as a group, then that's all that matters. Winning is all that matters to me. And I'm at the highest-level winning right now."

That's legit and, yes, the right attitude that great players need to have. But consider this: in the summer of 2016, when he was a free agent looking to score big on the market, he got basically frozen out. Teams that had cap space spent it on other players; no team that really "needed" a point guard could find the $30 million in cap space to pay him. He was acutely interested in joining the Minnesota Timberwolves as a free agent that summer, but that franchise traded for relative journeyman Ricky Rubio and decided not to venture into the NBA's punitive luxury tax system to pay Lowry, who under the rules of the time would have cost them about $3 in tax payments for every $1 on his contract.

It pissed him off no end, and while he ended up accepting a three-year deal worth $100 million in Toronto, he was not pleased. Oh, he knew that at the time he was the second-highest-paid point guard in the NBA behind Golden State's Stephen Curry (a point he made in a private conversation with me the day the Raptors announced his return), but he was still miffed.

The craziest thing about Lowry is that he's going to go down as one of, if not *the,* greatest players in franchise history and certainly one of its most successful, with multiple all-star selections and a championship on his résumé despite the fact that he was close to being run out of town on two occasions.

In 2013, the Raptors were basically at a crossroads. They had done nothing in years, and were trying to decide between building around Lowry, DeMar DeRozan, and coach Dwane Casey or tearing the team down to the foundation and basically starting over. In December, general manager Masai Ujiri seemed intent on blowing it up when he made a monstrous deal with the Sacramento Kings to ship Rudy Gay out of town for bits and pieces that might hasten a rebuild when they left. Lowry was seemingly the next to go; Toronto had a deal in place with New York to move him to the Knicks for Metta World Peace, Iman Shumpert, and draft picks that was hours from being completed.

"That deal was done," Lowry once said.

It fell apart at the last minute because the Knicks got cold feet, afraid of being fleeced by Ujiri, and it turned out to be one of the best deals the Raptors ever didn't make. Toronto, with Lowry at the helm, made the playoffs every year from 2013 forward. They became one of the most consistently successful franchises in the NBA, and Lowry, the miserable young man, turned into the face of the franchise and its heart.

The most down I've ever seen him was after he'd had a potential series-winning shot blocked at the end of the 2014 first-round series against Brooklyn, his first playoff appearance as a Raptor. He lay on the court, inconsolable after Toronto lost, but I also thought at that time that he'd won everyone over, that he cared so damn much and wanted everyone to see it. He might not have won the series but he won over any remaining doubters.

Then almost lost them, though.

In the middle of the 2019 championship season, Lowry was still bristling about the trade that sent his best friend DeMar DeRozan to San Antonio for Kawhi Leonard, and he was not totally engaged for some of the season. He didn't practice particularly hard or particularly willingly. He'd be there every day but he hadn't entirely bought in. He was pissed at Ujiri, pissed at his lot in life, and there was a feeling he was going off the radar. He sat with Ujiri in a meeting just before the NBA's February 2019 trade deadline, and there was every chance he'd be moved. Ujiri had talked to a handful of teams about him—Memphis among them in a much more elaborate trade that got Toronto Marc Gasol—but first the team president and star player had to chat.

"It was a well-needed conversation. It was a very professional conversation and it had to be done. We had to get everything on the table. Listen, 'Let's have this conversation, let's get everything out on the table and move on.' And that's what grown men do.

They have conversations, they figure it out, and you move on," Lowry once said.

"It wasn't a 'fuck you, fuck you.' It wasn't me asking, 'Hell, you want to trade me?' At the end of the day, he's going to make the decisions, right? I'm going to play no matter what it is. It was about making myself the best player that I can possibly be and getting on the same page about what he needs from me to be the best player—and vice versa. Just getting on the same page."

Much of Lowry's mistrust of authority and eagerness to challenge those in charge comes from his background and knowing that nothing can ever be taken for granted. He grew up tough on the north side of Philadelphia, raised by his mom and his grandmother, and realizing that he had to be strong or be swallowed up by the streets. It toughened him as a youth, it turned him into a hard man who fought for what he wanted.

"What my mom had to go through and my grandmom had to go through, feeding myself, my brother and my cousin and my little cousin and my other little cousins. Going to work, getting up at five in the morning and going to work and making me cereal, having a bowl of cereal sitting in the refrigerator with some milk and being able to provide for me and my brother and my family," he said during Toronto's championship run, "that's pressure. That's pressure to me. Just being willing to do whatever it takes to make sure that your kid will see better than what you've ever seen. Getting up and taking public transportation an hour and a half away. People like that are heroes to me—just going to work and grinding and doing whatever it takes to provide for your family."

Through all that prickliness and contrarianism and pain-in-the-ass persona that Lowry showed while helping the Raptors go from

NBA afterthought to NBA champions, at some deep level, he's a good and thoughtful man.

He revels in not playing the game, in goofing with the media every now and then by giving short shrift to interview sessions when it strikes him, by marching to his own tempo and to hell with what people think. He's a pain, he knows it, he plays it up, he uses it to his advantage when he doesn't want to do something.

But, at his heart? He's not soft but he's softer than he lets on.

It was sometime in the middle of that 2019 championship season and I needed a private word with him after a game-day shootaround for a story I was working on. Getting one-on-one time with Lowry was always a dicey proposition. He thinks that if he has to do media, he may as well talk to a big group rather than an individual because it's easier for him.

So it was with a bit of trepidation that I got a member of the Raptors media relations staff to stop him at the bottom of the hallway that leads from the court to the locker room door with the message that I needed a private moment. Waved down to the bottom of the ramp, I had no idea what to expect.

"Doug, you almost died on the job," he said, harkening to a heart episode that had knocked me out for months just about eight months earlier. "I always got time for you. I ain't gonna tell you shit, but I always got time for you."

A kind-hearted pain in the ass. Gotta love him.

20

TOUGH DECISIONS

By all accounts, the 2017–18 season was one to celebrate. The Toronto Raptors, the franchise that had trotted out so many mediocre teams over the years, made the playoffs for the fifth consecutive season and set a franchise record with 59 wins during the regular season, finishing with the number-one seed in the Eastern Conference. It felt as though the Raptors were finally ready to punch through in the playoffs. A finals appearance, once a pipe dream, now felt realistic.

And yet, when we look back at that magical season, all we'll remember is how the entire season went up in flames in less than a week. The Raptors faced off against LeBron James and the Cleveland Cavaliers for the third consecutive season. Two years earlier, the Cavs had won in six games in the Eastern Conference finals. The year before, James and the Cavs had swept the Raptors in the second round.

This year was going to be different. The Raptors had home court advantage. They were the more cohesive unit. The Cavs barely made it past the first round, needing a full seven games to get past a young and inexperienced Indiana Pacers squad. No matter what Toronto accomplished in the regular season, the team knew they had to get past James in order to finally conquer their playoff demons.

Without question, James was in the Raptors' heads a little bit. Even as the number-one seed, they recognized that it would take a confluence of events to get past him in a seven-game series. With home court advantage, Game 1 at home was paramount. Strange to say a number one–seeded team faced a must-win in the very first game of what many anticipated to be a long series, but Toronto needed that win to prevent all their past playoff doubts from rising to the surface again.

It looked like they were well on their way. The Raptors controlled most of the game and had a double-digit lead in the fourth quarter. But the Cavs chipped away, and the Raptors couldn't put them away. The final possession of regulation was excruciating. With a chance to win, the Raptors missed four potential game-winning shots, including a wide-open three from Fred VanVleet with mere seconds left on the clock. The team looked deflated after that possession, and lost 113–112 in overtime. The series wasn't over after one game, but in a way, it was. Game 2 was an even more embarrassing performance, a blowout loss at home that sent the Raptors into a hole they ultimately couldn't dig out of.

I wasn't at that game; I watched it from a hospital bed after some heart surgery. But I remember thinking, as those series of shots were missed and there was a sinking "here we go again" feeling, that Ujiri would be livid at the outcome, and if the series didn't turn around, he might do something big because he'd had enough. It wasn't ever that he didn't like Casey or DeRozan, but I knew him; I had an idea of how he thought and I knew what his mood would be if the inevitable happened.

If the team's spirit had been broken from losing the first two games at home, the official nail in the coffin came in Game 3 back in Cleveland when James hit a game-winning jumper at the buzzer over OG Anunoby. Two nights later, the most successful Raptors season ended in an embarrassing sweep. In the six years with the trio of head coach Dwane Casey and the all-star backcourt of Kyle Lowry and DeMar DeRozan, this was the highest they had reached but also the lowest.

It was hard to draw any conclusion from the sweep but this: the Raptors might have been the better team, but they just didn't have *the guy*. Changes were coming, but nobody could have expected what would happen that summer.

Because of how the season ended, Masai Ujiri knew he had to do something. You couldn't just keep knocking on the door over and over again with the same group, not after everything he had witnessed. He wasn't just disappointed in his players; there were also questions about the coaching staff. The entire organization was stunned by the result. There had been quiet confidence from the Raptors heading into the series.

After it all ended, just from talking to folks in the organization, you could feel the tension and the general consensus that the Raptors couldn't simply run it back again with the same group. Toronto had a lot of pressure heading into the second round against the Cavs, and Ujiri saw how his team reacted to that pressure. After the Game 3 loss, Ujiri and Casey got into a shouting match. The team had been building towards this showdown with James and the Cavs, and they'd completely folded.

Ujiri held a press conference shortly after the playoffs ended and said he would evaluate everything. He's never been the type of person to make a rash decision based on emotions, always choosing to take a step back to re-evaluate the big picture.

Ujiri had inherited Casey from the previous general manager, Bryan Colangelo. The two didn't have an organic partnership, but they worked through their differences. And over his seven seasons in Toronto, Casey had proved to be a really good head coach. Ujiri always thought Casey would get better at his job as the roster improved, and in many ways, especially in the regular season, that proved to be true. Ujiri valued consistency, and that's what Casey brought to the Raptors. There was a trust there, and both felt they were on the right path, even though there were lots of bumps in the playoffs. But after the Cleveland series, Ujiri took a hard look at the situation and concluded they had finally reached the end of the path with this group.

A few days after his end-of-season presser, Ujiri announced the firing of Casey, who ended up being named the Coach of the Year later in the summer. I was shocked by the decision, even though I admit it wasn't at all surprising once I had time to fully process it. I've been around enough teams to know when a head coach has run out of time. And to know when management has run out of patience. There were a lot of bitter feelings at the split. Casey is still angry at Ujiri to this day for the decision. He knew he had done a good job here, and he believed that if he had better players, he could have won bigger.

The decision to fire Casey was the biggest one Ujiri had to make so far in running this Raptors team, but it would just be the start of the most eventful summer in the franchise's history.

And the president knew it.

"Now it's my job. It's on me," Ujiri said the day he let Casey go. "Put it on me. Sometimes these things come to an end, our relationship came to an end and we'll figure out a way to move on, a new voice, and just new everything, in terms of that position."

With the firing of their head coach, Ujiri had made one thing clear: the Raptors were now all-in to win a championship. Those 59 wins in the regular season weren't enough anymore. Having home court advantage throughout the playoffs wasn't enough anymore. A conference finals appearance wouldn't suffice. For all the talk about the culture and the tight-knit family approach of this Raptors team, there was now a more ruthless reality: tough decisions had to be made to give the Raptors a serious chance at competing for a championship.

Hiring a new coach wasn't going to solve all the problems. The roster had proven that they were not capable of getting over the hump in the playoffs. DeMar DeRozan was the face of the Raptors' franchise, the teenager from Compton who embraced the city and told anyone who would listen that his goal was to spend his entire career in Toronto—something unheard of from anyone wearing a Raptors uniform. His loyalty to the city, and the way he improved year to year on the court, made him the perfect guy to lead the Raptors.

But to win a championship, you needed *the guy*, and there are only a handful of those guys in the entire world. The Raptors had seen it up close. James had toyed with them over and over again in the post-season. Ujiri had always pushed DeRozan to become that guy. He always asked his star guard to be more tough-minded, to be a hard-ass competitor. Ujiri gave DeRozan the keys to the franchise. To DeRozan's credit, he always came back each off-season improved. He became a better ball handler, a better shooter, and a better leader in the locker room over time.

At some point, I think Ujiri realized that no matter how much DeRozan improved, he wasn't going to become *the guy* on a championship. But despite his flaws, Ujiri might have continued tinkering the roster around DeRozan to make up for his shortcomings. Every team would love to acquire *the guy* who can be the number-one guy on a championship team, but they don't just fall from trees. That is why, when Ujiri and DeRozan spoke at summer league after the season, there was zero indication that he was going to be traded. Ujiri had given DeRozan the impression that he was going to be part of next year's team. They discussed the things Ujiri wanted DeRozan to work on during his summer workouts.

But things change in this league. While I do think the whole situation could have been handled better, I don't think Ujiri had any idea when he talked to DeRozan that a superstar was going to become available to them in the market. Kawhi Leonard was the 2014 NBA finals MVP and two-time Defensive Player of the Year. But he also played only nine games the season prior because of injury, and after a falling out with the Spurs, he demanded a trade.

A superstar of Leonard's calibre is rarely available in trades, which is why his availability came with plenty of caveats. The injury history was a concern. There was also the question of how confident his uncle Dennis was, who seemed to be dictating where Leonard's next NBA destination was going to be. There were rumblings he wanted to land in Los Angeles, with either the Lakers or Clippers. On top of it, any team trading for Leonard would only have him for one year before he hit unrestricted free agency in the summer.

There were a lot of risks involved in any trade for Leonard, but this was exactly the kind of player Ujiri knew the Raptors needed to give themselves a chance at winning a championship. And so, DeRozan, along with Jakob Pöltl, was dealt to the Spurs in exchange for Leonard and Danny Green.

"When I met with Aaron [Goodwin, one of DeRozan's agents] at summer league, maybe my mistake was saying there was nothing imminent at the time," Ujiri said in the aftermath of that trade. "I acknowledge that. If it was a mistake, I apologize to them, but at the time, we were fourth in the ranks of trying to get anything done [involving Leonard and the Spurs] and I didn't see anywhere where the talks were going. That's the message I delivered. It's my job to always go to these guys and always talk about the team as it is."

The basketball world was stunned. DeRozan felt blindsided. He had committed himself to Toronto and the Raptors organization. He had just spoken with Ujiri days before. And now he was off to San Antonio. I completely understand DeRozan's frustration with Ujiri, and the two have since made amends, but we're always reminded of how this basketball thing is a business. I always say this: sometimes what is true one day isn't true the next. It's an unpredictable business.

A lot of fans and even local media members didn't understand the move. The Raptors traded away a guy who wanted to be here, maybe the only guy of DeRozan's calibre who ever said that about the organization. But this was a new landscape now for the Raptors. The trade spoke to two things.

One, it spoke to DeRozan's development as a player over the years. He turned himself into a star player who was good enough that the Spurs would want him in such a blockbuster trade. It's a testament to all the hard work he and the organization put in.

Two, it told us everything we needed to know about Ujiri. He's a kind, gentle person, a great humanitarian, and lights up every room he is in, but he is also a ruthless competitor. If giving up the face of the franchise was going to give the Raptors a chance, even if it was a one-year window, to bring a championship to Toronto, he was going to take that risk.

In one summer, the Raptors as we knew them had transformed. They had a new head coach in Nick Nurse and a new star player in Kawhi Leonard. It was a necessary gamble. The Raptors had come close so many times in the playoffs, but they never got over the hump. The trade felt risky at the time, and truthfully, nobody knew what to expect, because Nurse had never coached at the NBA level, even though he was a basketball lifer, and even though Leonard already had a championship on his résumé, there were plenty of questions about his health and whether he even wanted to put on a Raptors uniform at all.

The Raptors had been one of the best success stories in the NBA for half a decade, emerging from the doldrums of mediocrity to become one of the most consistent franchises in the league. But they were missing one thing: the championship.

Some will say it wasn't Casey or DeRozan's fault, and that nobody was going to get past James and the Cavs anyway. After all, this guy won eight straight Eastern Conference final titles and three championships before leaving to join the Los Angeles Lakers. The Raptors weren't the only team who had their seasons ended by James over and over. It was a mountain that no one could get over in the East. But the sweep to the Cavs also revealed a lot of things about this Raptors team that made Ujiri confront the reality that a change was no longer optional, but necessary.

With two huge moves in the summer, they were now hopeful that they finally had the right group to get them over the hump.

21

KAWHI LEONARD

It was stunning Raptors news that broke in the pre-dawn hours of July 18, 2018—incomprehensible news in some ways to fans who'd grown used to much the same roster and many of the same stars over half a decade of consistent winning—and it was the most earth-shattering, sea-changing transaction in the history of the franchise in so many different ways.

We were all awoken to find out that Raptors president Masai Ujiri had gone all-in in his pursuit of the ultimate goal by trading away the iconic DeMar DeRozan, a young big man in Jakob Pöltl, and a draft pick to the San Antonio Spurs for Kawhi Leonard and Danny Green.

Pöltl, the pick, and Green were truly afterthoughts. The trade in everyone's mind was DeRozan for Leonard, and it was bigger than any deal ever. The alerts on my phone began in the middle of the night, and by about 5 a.m. I was at the kitchen table madly typing updates as information came in.

Leonard? The unknown star from the Spurs who had missed all

but nine games of the previous season because of a lingering, mysterious leg injury?

Leonard? Whose reputation around the league was in tatters because there were those who thought he was a malingerer who had given up on one of the most respected franchises in the league?

Leonard? The antithesis of DeRozan, quiet and mysterious and not at all interested in the machinations of NBA fame, which said the best players would use their skills to enhance their brands?

Leonard?

Hell, one of the first reactions was that it was likely he wouldn't even report to Toronto, that he wanted to go play in his hometown of Los Angeles and that a snowy, cold, foreign city and a franchise that hadn't really done anything was about the last place he wanted to spend the final season of the contract he was operating under.

Leonard? For DeRozan, the beloved Raptor lifer who had announced his return at one point by saying: "I am Toronto"?

Oh yeah, this was never, ever going to work out. I was dubious. The immediate reaction was that it was a crushing blow to DeRozan, whom I very much respected and liked and with whom I had a tremendous relationship, but it was certainly an easily defensible basketball move. I had seen Leonard win championships with the San Antonio Spurs, I knew how good he could be, but there were so many questions. His health, whether he'd even want to be in Toronto, and how he would fit into a new team were all legitimate concerns I had immediately, and maybe they were unfounded in the end, but they were real.

Except that it did work out—and better than anyone could have expected in those early days when the shock waves of the deal were rumbling through the basketball world.

It was to Leonard's credit that he was the first to reach out privately to the most important new teammate he had, to soothe hard feelings and start with a clean slate.

Kyle Lowry took the trade of DeRozan, his best friend and for six seasons his closest teammate, exceptionally hard. We all did to some degree. It was like a family member being banished and there were hurt feelings. Raptors president Masai Ujiri had broken up the most successful duo in franchise history in a brutal bit of necessary business and Lowry was displeased. He didn't know Leonard as anything other than an opponent for a couple of games each season, and Lowry had heard the second-hand rumblings of Leonard's dissatisfaction with the trade.

But, in a telling move that no one found out about for months, Leonard extended the first olive branch, reaching out by text to tell Lowry he understood his anger and disappointment but vowing to make things work.

No one knew about it for months, but it was maybe the first sign that Leonard was not this oddball monster some thought him to be. And that he was and would be a good teammate. There were those in San Antonio who took shots at him as he sat out much of the 2017–18 season, most notably the much-respected Tony Parker, who had chastised Leonard publicly for seeking outside medical advice.

"I had options, too, obviously; when you have a big injury like that you can go to L.A., Europe, France," Parker famously said late in that season, the final straw that ensured Leonard would be gone. "I could've gone anywhere, but I trust my Spurs doctors. They have been with me my whole career . . . I didn't take two weeks to go through options. For me, it was a no-brainer because I feel like we have the best medical team in the world."

But with one text to Lowry, Leonard made a huge statement.

"When he texted me, it was a quick text and just showed the type of person he is," Lowry would say. "Willing to reach out, understanding that this situation was a little bit sensitive. But he knew that he felt something could be done special with our group."

While Leonard had reached out to Lowry, he hadn't made any public appearances, and so his first news conference in Toronto—at media day about two months after the trade had been consummated—was one of the most anticipated in franchise history. We didn't know even if he'd show up, or how he would react to what were the first questions he faced. We knew nothing about his interaction with large crowds of media, and it could have been a make-or-break situation.

As the old guy on the beat, I knew I'd have the chance to ask the first question, and I thought about the tone, the substance that entire morning. I figured the great unknown about Leonard was just that: he was unknown. And what better way to break the ice, perhaps learn something, than to let him tell us what he was like? No one knew him better than he did, so give him his shot.

A perfectly logical question that turned into a season-long phenomenon when he finished his answer by telling us all, with a chuckle and laugh that would become a viral sensation:

"I'm a fun guy."

What he went on to do was unprecedented, historic, memorable. Being along for the ride was a treat, one of those years that more than made up for the expansion seasons, the disappointment of not being able to get past LeBron James and the Cleveland Cavaliers in the mid-2010s, all those losses and all those early endings to seasons.

Memorable for all. The Raptors ended up having one of the best regular seasons in franchise history, 58 wins despite Leonard resting for a quarter of them. It was a delicate balancing act of keeping him healthy and letting the team grow, and it took cooperation from everyone. His teammates understood he had to be handled differently and their acceptance of that made it easier for everyone. And for Leonard.

"Without a doubt," Raptors coach Nick Nurse would say months after the trade for Leonard, "the best thing about this thing is that somehow I wound up on the sideline getting to watch this guy play up close."

Nurse's opinion was one shared by anyone who got to watch Leonard play regularly in one tremendous season, to see his understated brilliance, his stoic determination, his ability to affect a game offensively and defensively. In Game 5 of the Eastern Conference final against Milwaukee, with the series tied 2–2, Leonard just took over. He made shots and made brilliant defensive plays; it was a tour de force reminiscent of something Michael Jordan might have done in his heyday.

Leonard had that ability to take over a game. He had a presence.

He ended the year as the Most Valuable Player of the NBA finals, the second time in his career he'd won that honour; he led the Raptors in their most memorable run ever and, counter to what so many had thought, he was not this recalcitrant contrarian who didn't want to be where he was.

As a player, he had no equal in the first 25 years of the Raptors' existence. He was only in Toronto for one season, so it's hard to figure where he might fit on an "all-time Raptors" team because longevity is such an integral part of that discussion, but suffice it to say, it was delightful to watch him.

He was tough and dogged and went about dominating games

without much of the flash of his other great peers, but that was part of the pleasure of watching him. He worked and worked hard and worked his craft with maniacal attention to detail and that set him apart. Nick Nurse told us repeatedly through the season that Leonard's professionalism is what stood out. He put in an honest day's work every day, lifting weights, getting treatment, watching film, whatever was called for. You could see it trickle down to his teammates, young players like Fred VanVleet and Pascal Siakam who took their cues from Leonard, something that became more evident as the 2019–20 season unfolded.

And in many ways, Leonard and the Raptors changed the NBA forever, which might end up being his greatest legacy. Because of the lingering leg injury—one that he sought treatment for from his own team of physicians and athletic trainers, away from the Spurs' own medical staff—the Raptors handled him differently, giving him nearly a quarter of the 82-game season off for what was termed "load man-agement." It was the perfect treatment plan; Leonard felt engaged and involved in all facets of his recovery, and it eased the transition to Toronto considerably. He trusted the people around him and that was in stark contrast with how he felt in his final season with the Spurs.

"We've been doing a great job of making sure that nothing flares up or gets out of control. It's just been great. I'm just happy that I'm able to play . . . It's amazing. I feel good and we have something to look forward to," he said during the season.

And because he felt comfortable and respected and informed and involved, it made him a better fit. All those worries about how he'd like Toronto, how he would deal with a new franchise, a new city, a new medical team, new coaches, and new teammates disappeared, and maybe he wasn't a public cheerleader or a talkative leader, but he certainly wasn't the aloof loner many had thought he was on the night of the trade.

The one thing about Leonard that ran counter to what everyone expected of him was how he handled the media responsibilities that came with his status on the team.

He was far from verbose—why use 20 words when five would suffice?—but there wasn't a time when he steadfastly refused to talk either after a game or after a practice. He might not say anything of significance and he always seemed to be perturbed by having to answer the same question posed in a different fashion in the same media scrum, but he would stand there and talk for a few minutes whenever the media needed him.

He could be quite unintentionally funny in the way he took every question literally. His being a "fun guy" and his laugh became a running joke from his first media session to his last public appearance at the championship parade.

It wasn't necessary to speak to him after every game—those who covered the team regularly were smart and veteran enough to know that repeated requests would eventually lead to Leonard shutting down completely and there was no reason to push things.

But when we needed him, he'd talk. He would answer questions quite literally and there was no idle chit-chat. He tired of being asked the same question twice and would give us lines like "As I just said" that were signals he was getting fed up with that night's scrum. No animosity but no engagement.

It was a dance—the post-game quotes in the regular season were hardly illuminating or earth-shattering and we'd all probably have been better off finding other ways to describe what happened—but he'd do the dance when he needed to.

Leonard was, in fact, just continuing a long tradition in which the best players on the team understood and accepted their media responsibilities.

Damon Stoudamire took losses as hard as any player to ever wear a Raptors uniform, but the team's first star would stand there after every game and try to explain what had happened to cause an overmatched expansion team to lose. Vince Carter, one of the most popular players on the planet in his Toronto heyday, would talk after every practice, every shootaround, every game, and he might not say anything of substance but he'd say it for the cameras and our stories. Chris Bosh used to make us wait forever as he meticulously dressed and tied his tie and put in his earrings, and then he'd answer questions patiently. DeMar DeRozan was a gem, always willing to fulfill his obligations.

In many ways, Toronto reporters have been lucky, and Leonard, despite what we'd heard and what we'd expected, was the same as those who went before him.

The funny thing with Leonard was that he ended his Toronto tenure offering some wonderful insight into his personality, his drive, his life. It was as if his large media gatherings at the NBA finals were somehow cathartic; he opened up like he seldom had in front of the largest groups of reporters of the season. It ran counter to what we'd seen all year but he showed how willing he could be to share his private thoughts. We'd tried to draw him out in quick post-game scrums but it was frustrating. He never seemed like an "open" interview subject. It was frustrating because we'd been used to the best players on the team—Stoudamire, Carter, Bosh, DeRozan—being fine interviews. Leonard was just different during the finals.

"Well, just the year, last year, a lot of people were doubting me," he said in one memorable post-game session during the championship series against Golden State. "They thought I was either faking an injury or didn't want to play for a team. That was disappointing to me that that was out in the media, because I love the game of basketball. Like I always say, if we're not playing this game, if we're hurt, I mean, you're down. So me just going through that, and I just knew that I would have to make myself happy and no one else. And I have to trust myself. And whatever, it doesn't matter what anybody has to say about me. I know who I am as a person, I know how I feel, and always just trust yourself.

"And that was my goal and my focus. I don't care about what the media has to say about me or if they want me to score or whatever, 30 points, because I did the game before, I'm going to come out and play the right way, I'm not trying to make headlines. And that's just things that I pretty much learned just throughout this journey of being in the NBA. So that's how I just keep growing up as a man and that's why I say, I just think about my past life and try to learn from situations and be wise and learn from others."

It is that past life that, in many ways, shaped the man Leonard became. He was just 16 years old—a very good high school basketball star in the hard Compton area of Los Angeles but not someone who anyone expected would grow into one of the best players in the world—when his father, Mark Leonard, known to all as "Mick," was gunned down and murdered in a still-unsolved crime outside the car wash he owned and had devoted his life to building.

It was an unimaginable tragedy—a senseless, brazen late-day murder of a family man who was rushing through work that day so he could go watch his son play a game about an hour away in the choking Los Angeles traffic—and its impact on Kawhi cannot be measured. He seldom opens up about it but we knew it was part of his background, part of his being, and it took until the last weeks of his time in Toronto for him to fully explain or at least try to explain what it did to him. What it made him. What it meant to him.

"Once it happened, I thought about it a lot," he said one night during the finals. "But as I got older, I pretty much just really stopped thinking about it. I think it just gave me a sense and feel that life and basketball are two different things and just really enjoy your time and moments. Like I always say, this is basketball; just go out there and have fun. These are going to be the best years of my life, playing this game.

"Being 27, this young, you shouldn't be stressing in life about things that really don't matter. As long as your family is healthy, you're able to see the people that you love, and you're able to walk, run, you're not injured. So all those things go into account. Go out here, lay it all out on the floor, do the best job I could possibly do and try to win."

It's what he did and what he was supposed to do, and for all we ask of sports stars outside of the game, demanding and expecting they will be open and conversant and welcoming of the scrutiny that comes with their place in the sports world, isn't that enough?

Who cares, really, about all the extraneous stuff? Does it matter when there is athletic brilliance to watch on nearly a nightly basis? Isn't the big obligation just to be as good a player and teammate as you can be? His teammates liked him, that's all that mattered. He won and he worked hard and gave an honest effort every time out, and does the rest even matter?

It would have been nice if he joked and chatted with us in a personal manner but it wasn't necessary.

It was about basketball, and in that regard, the magical year of Kawhi Leonard was all it was supposed to be.

22

DWANE AND NICK

In early January, a few months into the 2019 season, the Toronto Raptors flew to San Antonio for Kawhi Leonard's much-anticipated return. He was greeted with boos from the moment he took the floor in warm-ups, and the San Antonio crowd didn't let up from there. That evening, Spurs fans got to celebrate a victory over a player they had thought would take the baton from David Robinson and Tim Duncan before him and be the centrepiece of a championship contending team for the next decade. The Spurs won in a rout, beating the Raptors 125–107.

From the outside, it felt like the Raptors were trying to keep everything together. Even with the loss, Toronto was 28–12 and looking like a contender once again in the East. But there were plenty of questions surrounding the team about its chemistry, especially with Leonard's load management causing him to miss seemingly every other game and the fact that everyone was proceeding with the expectation that they had one full season to come together and make a run at the title as Leonard's free agency loomed.

And then there was Kyle Lowry. On his best day, Lowry's mood can still be unpredictable. From media day, he seemed to make a point of letting everyone know that he still wasn't happy about losing his best friend DeMar DeRozan to a trade. Lowry is a professional, and he showed up to play every night. You could never question his effort, but was he happy? A month into the season, Lowry sat down with ESPN's Rachel Nichols for a one-on-one interview and basically confirmed that he and Masai Ujiri hadn't spoken at length since the trade.

I wanted to know how Lowry was really feeling, beyond what he was telling the media. A day earlier, I pulled DeRozan aside for a chat after his first scrum with Toronto reporters since his trade. "How's Kyle doing?" I asked. DeRozan's response: "It's a much better situation for him. There is no noise."

I think that pretty much summed up the difference between Dwane Casey and Nick Nurse.

Casey was a great guy and one of the nicest gentlemen I've met in the game of basketball. He took the Raptors franchise and moulded it into a consistent winning team. He helped lay the foundation that would ultimately result in a championship. He treated everyone with respect and as equals, and to this day, I consider him a friend. He and DeRozan will be forever linked, and DeRozan knows what Casey did for him.

"I think Casey was patient with me," DeRozan once told me. "I wouldn't say hard, I wouldn't say soft; he was patient with me. He allowed me to be me and he allowed me to make mistakes and correct my mistakes, or allowed me to figure out the mistakes I would make and correct them myself. At the end of the day, he seen how much I loved the game and cared and wanted to be good. To have a coach that didn't really enforce nothing on you was great for me."

But when one coach is replaced with another, all you notice are the differences. Fair or not, that's how the game goes. The new coach is often brought in because he has qualities that the former coach didn't have.

Nurse was publicly as laid-back as they came, a stark contrast to Casey, who reacted more emotionally in the way he dealt with players and with high-pressure games. It created a sense of stress and extra pressure that trickled down to the players. You could feel it. Sometimes you could see it. Not every coach is perfect, and every situation demands a different kind of temperament, especially in the NBA. There was "noise" sometimes.

The hard-nosed, demanding approach worked really well when the Raptors needed to develop winning habits and turn themselves from a team out of the playoff race to a perennial contender for the number-one seed in the East. But now the Raptors had done everything, except win the championship. And to get to the promised land, they tapped Nurse to be their head coach to lead them there.

Nurse had been an assistant coach with the Raptors for five years. Before that, he was a basketball vagabond, with a coaching résumé spanning several continents. After Casey was fired, the Raptors immediately honed in on Mike Budenholzer, who came from the Spurs' coaching system and had a stellar run in Atlanta as their head coach. But the Raptors had questions about Budenholzer, and they weren't answered, at least not to Ujiri's or the organization's liking during the extensive interview process. Culture is a huge factor for the Raptors, and they ultimately decided Budenholzer wasn't the right fit.

Other candidates were interviewed after Budenholzer took the

Milwaukee Bucks' head coaching gig, but the Raptors soon honed in on Nurse. They were familiar with him, but like I've always said, the hardest adjustment for a coach is going from the assistant coach's chair, shifting one spot to the head coaching seat.

The move to hire Nurse was arguably as bold as it was to fire Casey and to trade for Leonard. I was surprised. Even when he was an assistant to Casey, Nurse wasn't the lead assistant or the go-to guy on the staff. Honestly, when they made the hire, I felt like the Raptors had settled. It was a ballsy move because this was a guy that people around the league respected, but no one had any idea how he would be as an NBA head coach. In Toronto, fans demanded a "name" coach, maybe someone like Jeff Van Gundy, or his brother Stan, or any of the dozen other lifers looking for work with a promising team accustomed to success.

Traditionally, a team like the Raptors who were trying to get over the playoff hump looked towards someone with experience and a proven résumé in the NBA. Nurse had won everywhere he coached, but did it really make sense to throw a first-time NBA head coach into this situation? Remember, the hiring happened before the Leonard trade. Acquiring the former Spurs star only made this situation even more challenging.

The biggest thing that stood out to Ujiri during the interview process, and something they already knew because of his time with the Raptors coaching staff, was Nurse's in-game creativity. And more importantly, it was his laid-back demeanour. Nurse has a confidence about him and he's rarely ruffled by things that happen during and between games. He was a guy who wouldn't get worked up about the little things and was always trying to figure out how things went wrong and how to make them right.

If there was a criticism of Casey's tenure here, it was his rigidness. The Raptors wanted someone who would be more malleable and adaptable to situations as they arose in the playoffs, where each series, each game, each quarter, and each possession demands on-the-fly adjustments. They thought Nurse was the perfect person to handle those pressure situations.

They wanted someone who would help this team block out the noise and bring calm to what would be a high-pressure environment. The familiarity with the roster helped. He had relationships with all of these guys. Incorporating Leonard was a priority, but getting on the same page with Lowry was essential to putting this team on track for a championship push.

Casey's relationship with Lowry evolved over the years. Lowry had arrived in Toronto with a bit of a reputation as someone who never got along with his coaches. When he first got here, Casey tried to butt heads with Lowry too. It was just in Casey's nature, and Lowry never walked away from a back-and-forth either. Credit to Casey and Lowry. They realized that in order to succeed, they needed each other. The relationship grew.

In the early years, Casey would tell us privately that he thought Lowry would rip the team apart, that he would pit one side of the locker room against the other and destroy what they were trying to build. The two found common ground, though, and a respect for each other. They were both competitive guys who needed to get on the same page. Over time, Casey realized he had to let Lowry rant and vent and be a pain in the ass because it helped bring out the best version of him on the court.

If the Raptors were going to win, Casey knew he couldn't get in Lowry's face all the time. Once he realized that and let Lowry be, the team started to flourish. Publicly, Lowry also started praising his head coach, and vice versa. That was one of Casey's best attributes: he figured out how to deal with his players along the way. For all the criticisms about how he was not adaptable as a game strategist, you could definitely not say the same about Casey the people-manager.

Nurse didn't have the same runway to build a relationship with Lowry, and after all, what was more important was getting Lowry and Leonard on the same page on the court. A mid-season meeting between Lowry and Ujiri helped clear the air, and everyone agreed to set their differences aside for the common goal: bringing the Larry O'Brien Trophy to Toronto. In a way, you have to credit Casey for preparing Lowry for this moment. He had come a long way since arriving in Toronto.

Over the course of the season, the Raptors started taking on the calm and confident personality of their best player, Leonard, but also of their new head coach. There was no noise. Nurse was easygoing. He earned the respect of his players with his X's and O's. His confidence permeated through the locker room just as equally as Leonard's.

I can't think of a more challenging situation for a rookie NBA head coach to walk into, and Nurse handled it perfectly. He answered every question about Leonard's load management and questions surrounding his health and game-to-game availability. On the court, he used the regular season to experiment with different lineups. He managed through different injuries, different roster iterations, and when the Raptors acquired Marc Gasol at the trade deadline, Nurse handled sending Serge Ibaka—who was having a magnificent season—to the bench in place of Gasol perfectly. Sacrifices are made on every championship team, but they're also only made when the players believe in what their coach is doing.

There's no question the relationship between Casey and Nurse was fractured. They weren't the closest of friends when they worked together, but Casey was angry at Ujiri for his firing, and watching his assistant coach get his job couldn't have made him feel any better. A bit of that anger was transferred to Nurse. It's completely understandable that Casey would feel that way. He had a hard road coming up in the game of basketball, he's lived a tough life, worked as hard as anyone, and then he watched as the Raptors hired a guy who had never been a head coach at the NBA level to replace him.

Casey ended up taking the head coaching job in Detroit. The Pistons beat the Raptors all three times during the regular season. Whenever he could, Casey would be quick to remind everyone of the success the Raptors had while he was here. It was an awkward situation for everyone.

I don't think Nurse and Casey have spoken since they lost together to the Cavaliers in the 2018 playoffs. It's unclear if they'll ever speak again. Nurse has handled it well. At every chance, he's praised Casey publicly and has never said a bad word about him privately. You couldn't say the same for Casey. He would privately criticize and rip his former assistant. It felt like Casey needed to defend what he had helped build here in Toronto and remind people of his record with the Raptors.

Do I think Casey will ever smooth things over with Nurse or Ujiri? I don't think so. And that's unfortunate, because they're all great guys. But sometimes shit happens in this business and it's bad shit, and it takes a long time for those wounds to heal. Casey and Nurse are both proud guys, so maybe it'll just take one of them to be the first to reach out to mend those hurt feelings.

In no way was Nurse working behind the scenes to have Casey

fired or to angle for his job. The opportunity came up, and when you have a chance to get one of 30 available NBA head coaching gigs, you take it. And when you're asked in the interview by management to explain why you're the right guy, you'll probably point out things that you believe you can do better than the last guy.

The Raptors weren't too concerned with how their former coach felt or if Lowry harboured any resentment towards management for trading his best friend. This was the cost of going for a championship. On your way to the top, you have to make some difficult decisions along the way, and if it all pays off, everybody can understand and rationalize the decisions afterwards.

Going into training camp, there had been a lot of uncertainty about the Raptors, and whether Nurse was the right coach was a major question mark. But he aced his first regular season with the team, navigating through everything and creating a sense of calm in what was a very high-pressure environment. The Raptors won 58 games, one short of their franchise-setting mark the year before.

But nobody cared.

This entire season was 82 practices, a buildup towards the playoffs, where we would find out whether Nurse and Leonard would help the Raptors finally get over all their past playoff failures.

23

THE TURNING POINT

The 2010–11 season was a low point for the Raptors franchise. Under the guidance of head coach Jay Triano, the team finished with a 22–60 record. It was their third straight losing season, and since Vince Carter's departure almost a decade earlier, Toronto had made the playoffs just twice. It had been 10 years since they got out of the first round.

During that period, the Raptors cycled through a series of head coaches. Out went Lenny Wilkens. In came Kevin O'Neill, who lasted all of one season before giving way to Sam Mitchell, who lasted less than five full seasons and even won a Coach of the Year award before giving way to Triano, who finished his Raptor tenure with an 87–142 record.

The team had watched their star Chris Bosh leave via free agency to join the Miami Heat. They were a young franchise in need of guidance.

A decade later, the Raptors would be NBA champions.

And you could say the turning point was when general manager

Bryan Colangelo picked up the phone and asked the Dallas Mavericks for permission to interview assistant head coach Dwane Casey.

It was a move that started the process of rescuing the Raptors from the cycle of mediocrity they were trapped in.

Casey might not have been a household name. He wasn't the kind of hire that would make national headlines. He started in the NBA as an assistant coach with the Seattle Supersonics in 1994, had a brief head-coaching stint with the Minnesota Timberwolves, and then joined the Mavericks in 2008.

In Dallas with Rick Carlisle's coaching staff, Casey developed a reputation as a well-respected tactician. He was known as one of the best in the game when it came to devising defensive schemes. When Casey accepted the Raptors job, it was days after the Mavericks upset LeBron James and the Heat in the 2011 NBA finals. Casey got credited with coming up with a game plan to contain the best player in the game.

Immediately after the hire, I got on the phone with Carlisle to talk about it. The Mavs coach was celebrating his championship with a trip to the Champs-Élysées.

"He's going to be perfect for Toronto," Carlisle told me. That he would take the time while on vacation to make a call to a reporter to tout the talents of a man who had just left his organization spoke volumes about how Casey was regarded. I had chatted with Dwane a fair amount while covering the Dallas–Miami NBA finals, the first real interaction I'd ever had with him, and he struck me as a good man, comfortable and confident in his abilities and personality.

Beyond the X's and O's, Carlisle knew the type of coach Casey was. Dwane was very single-minded in what he wanted from a team, Carlisle told me, and he never wavered from it. His word was his bond.

It sounded exactly like what the Raptors needed. They were perennially one of the worst defensive teams in the league, and Casey's task was to mould them into a more cohesive unit. The sheer force of his personality would eventually get through to the players, but this was the NBA, and if you wanted to see results on the court, you still needed enough talent to make it work. The Raptors didn't have that when Casey arrived. In his first season, the team won 23 games. The following year, they improved to 34–48 but still fell short of making the playoffs.

Casey wasn't discouraged. He recognized that this wouldn't happen overnight. This job required patience. The Raptors recognized that, too. They had changed coaches almost every other season, moved from one philosophy to the next. So Casey chipped away, day by day, to establish a new culture within the organization and hammer his point home.

To illustrate his point, Casey had Graeme McIntosh, an aide of Colangelo's, find a 1,300-pound rock from Northern Ontario. He placed the boulder just inside the front door to the team's locker room. The motto was "Pound the Rock," which Casey adapted from the San Antonio Spurs, the model of consistency in the NBA.

"The philosophy is, if you're a stonecutter, you're pounding that rock every day," Casey said of the credo that came from Jacob Riis. Riis is not a name normally associated with the NBA or any level of basketball, a photographer and journalist known for promoting urban reform at the turn of the 20th century. "No matter what walk of life you're in, whether you're a lawyer, doctor, janitor, construction worker, whatever you are, you have to pound the rock. The rock may not seem like it's going to crack. You may hit it 100 times, but on that 101st time, you'll crack it, but every day you've got to come in and hit it and challenge yourself to work at it and not give up," said Casey.

Every day, during games, at practice and shootarounds, and during film sessions, Casey kept reiterating the same points: hard work, defensive focus, playing for the guy sitting next to you as much as you play for yourself. The giant rock was a reminder of that every time they stepped into the locker room.

When we first found out about the rock, I admit it was a little weird. It felt like a new-age thing that didn't really make sense. A lot of us just didn't know what that was going to do for the team. But that's the thing with Casey. You spend enough time around him, whether as a player or a media member, and you come to appreciate his consistency.

The rock represented the core principles he believed in, and after a while, when players realized that this guy wasn't just bullshitting, the message started to get through. Hey, this guy isn't going to stop talking about these things. He's for real. So we're going to have to either buy in or play somewhere else.

Another thing about Casey: he was very personable and friendly, and he went to great lengths to make sure he learned the names of everyone working in the organization. He would even involve some of us media members. In his first couple seasons here in Toronto, I often woke up and saw a text message from Casey on my phone. I remember the inspirational messages he would send. "Find your belief and stick to it," one read.

I had no idea why I was getting these messages. Later, I found out he was actually group texting them to players and people in the organization, and somehow I found myself on the list as well.

One day, I asked Casey why I was getting these messages.

"We need people around the team to know what we're doing," he told me.

Casey was confident in his approach and wanted everyone to know what he was doing from the very start.

His third season with the team was when the results finally showed on the court. Masai Ujiri had taken over as the team's general manager, and after trading Rudy Gay to the Sacramento Kings in December of that season, the team took off.

Nobody could have seen it coming. It felt like a long rebuild was on its way. Kyle Lowry had one foot out the door and would have ended up on the New York Knicks if owner James Dolan hadn't gotten cold feet about losing another trade to Ujiri.

The trade to the Knicks fell apart, and the Raptors started looking like a completely different team. They began looking like a group who took after Casey's message and began playing more responsibly on the court. They went from a bunch of young guys who had no idea how to win to what Casey must have envisioned when he took this job. The Raptors finished with 48 wins and clinched a playoff berth.

That season, we started to see the development of Lowry and DeMar DeRozan as a formidable starting backcourt.

DeRozan was a young player still finding his way; he was willing to be taught, and Casey helped in his development. He kept preaching the same things: the consistency in effort and how to be more responsible as a basketball player. It finally got through to the players after some time.

DeRozan knows what Casey did for him, which was to work with him to allow a young unproven player to find his way and to flourish. It was an excellent coupling that allowed a struggling Raptors franchise to find consistent success for one of the few times in its history.

But Lowry had been around the league a bit longer than DeRozan, and as two strong-willed individuals, it took time for Casey and Lowry to get on the same page. When they did, this team took off. Still, when the Raptors lost to the Nets in the first round that season and were swept by the Washington Wizards in the first round the following season, questions grew about Casey's ability to get this team over the hump in the playoffs.

In 2016, the team made it to the Eastern Conference finals and came within two wins of making the NBA finals, but those questions remained. There have been criticisms about Casey's flexibility. I disagree with a lot of that. After each playoff disappointment, Casey always listened to Ujiri when he suggested different things, approaches on the court, changes to the coaching staff, and even a culture reset. Casey proved himself to be adaptable through it all. He allowed himself to change as a head coach in order to allow the team to grow.

Casey was smart enough to know that the game was changing. There was more emphasis on the three-point shot, and with different personnel, the Raptors needed to switch up their style to keep up with the modern game. His core beliefs never changed. He wanted his team to be defensive-minded and play disciplined basketball.

It's why Casey's tenure in Toronto lasted so long, even with those early-year struggles and playoff disappointments. When Ujiri took over from Colangelo, he could have easily picked his own coach, but Casey kept delivering results. Ujiri is a very demanding boss, and he made Casey work harder. There was a consistency to their belief in the team. The roster had grown together into a playoff team and then a contender in the East. Casey had won a championship in Dallas, and that earned the respect of his players, too. He, like Ujiri, championed the Raptors and always told the city of Toronto to believe in the team and their players.

After the team's embarrassing 2018 playoff exit, Ujiri decided it was time for a new voice, but that shouldn't take away from what Casey did for this Raptors franchise. Without the foundation that he laid, the team wouldn't have a championship banner hanging at Scotiabank Arena today.

He was by far the most competent head coach in franchise history. He built a culture and a program here. It was more than lip service. You only need to look at the team's record and the consecutive playoff appearances. He created this "us versus the world" mentality that became the We the North campaign. He kept convincing the players they would eventually turn the corner, and when they did, they listened to him some more.

Casey cared about his players and wanted them to be better. He genuinely cared about them as individuals not just for their value on the court, but as men he helped to raise. He treated everyone as people. Casey was there when DeRozan's kids were born. He would talk to the younger guys about taking care of their family. The players realized that and appreciated it.

When I was scheduled for my triple bypass in 2015, the night before surgery, I decided to cover a Raptors home game. I wanted to be with the team and be at a game one last time, knowing I was going to be in the hospital recovering for weeks. At the start of his post-game scrum, before answering any questions about the game, Casey said, "First of all, I want to wish Doug the best of luck." Those little moments meant a lot to me.

With Casey, there were plenty of those little moments that people who follow the team might not know about. When I missed the

2018 playoffs, the one that would get him fired, he texted me every day during the post-season while I was recuperating in the hospital. During the first-round series against the Washington Wizards, he and Ujiri both took the time to visit me in the hospital.

Casey would just sit there and we would just swap stories. This guy was coaching in the NBA playoffs; he didn't need to give a crap about a reporter who was away from the game. I didn't even work for the Raptors. But that was just the kind of guy he was.

A month later, he was out of a job. I was still in the hospital and didn't reach out to him. I wanted to give Casey some time, figured it was appropriate, especially since the season had fallen apart so fast and he was dealing with the fact that he had lost his job. He would still text me, not to vent, not to talk about his situation, but just to check in. It was a very considerate thing that I won't soon forget.

People always like to ask: What would have happened if he'd had a chance to coach Kawhi Leonard? Now, I don't know how he would have handled his best player missing a bunch of games in the regular season, but I would have liked to have found out. Casey could have very well led the Raptors to the championship as well.

I know he's pissed off about not having that chance. Imagine the things he could have done defensively with Leonard, Marc Gasol, and Danny Green. I mean, we don't have to imagine, we saw how great they were on the defensive end especially in the post-season.

These are the things I don't want people to forget about Casey. He came up short in getting them to a championship, but without him, none of this would have happened. He should be remembered as the head coach who helped turn a moribund franchise into a consistent winner.

That's the legacy Dwane Casey leaves behind in Toronto.

24

TWO SHOTS

Anyone who has ever picked up a basketball has dreamed about it.

Game 7.

The clock is ticking down.

Ball in your hand.

A shot for the win.

It always plays out so perfectly in our mind.

The ball swishes perfectly through the net.

You are the hero of this narrative every time.

In real life, those moments are much different. The tension of Game 7 often borders on uncomfortable. Teams rarely play their best games. The entire season—all those games you play, all those practices and late-night workouts—builds up to this single elimination game. Even for the best athletes in the world, the pressure is immense. It's something those of us who have followed the Raptors since their inception have almost come to expect. For a team that's only played in 19 playoff series in its first 25 years, the rate of Game 7s—or winner-take-all games in shorter series—is astonishing.

There was a deciding Game 5 in the first-round series against New York in 2001 and a Game 7 in the very next series. There was a dramatic Game 7 against the Brooklyn Nets in 2014 and two—the first round against Indiana and the conference semifinals against Miami—in 2016 before a rematch with the Sixers in the 2019 conference semifinals.

Some were close—the New York series was in doubt until the final minute, Game 7 against Brooklyn came down to the last second, and there was a five-point spread in the final game of the 2016 Indiana series—and all were tense.

But nothing tops the mirror-image ends to Toronto–Philadelphia games 18 years apart.

One shot can often change the course of a franchise's history.

For the Raptors, it was two shots.

Two game-winning attempts in Game 7.

Eighteen years apart.

The exact same scenario.

Against the same team.

Sports is weird sometimes.

The second-round series between Toronto and the Philadelphia 76ers was a classic. It was two of the biggest stars in the game, Vince Carter and Allen Iverson, trading heavyweight punches. Carter would score 50 points in a game. Iverson would respond with one of his own. The teams found themselves tied 3–3 apiece. A Game 7 in Philadelphia would decide the series.

The game was scheduled for Sunday afternoon, and on Friday evening, news started trickling out that Carter was planning on attending his graduation ceremony in North Carolina on the morning of the game.

A lot of us didn't really understand how that would work. In Canada, graduation ceremonies are day-long affairs. How would Carter be able to fly there and then play in the most pivotal game in the franchise's history?

As we got more details, it started to make more sense. Carter would fly to North Carolina in the morning and then take a private jet to Philadelphia and be back in time for the team's final walk-through before tipoff. In essence, he wasn't going to miss a thing.

Of course people still had questions. How would the same-day travel affect him physically and mentally? Was it a responsible decision to create a distraction on the eve of a Game 7? There was plenty of controversy around the decision, and a segment of Raptors fans remain upset with Carter to this day.

I never thought it was a big deal. This was the NBA. If you showed up to practice and played hard in games, what you did during your private time was entirely up to you. These were grown men and it was up to them to be responsible with that time.

I have no doubt other guys on the team spent the Saturday evening before the game going out for dinner, and maybe a few of them stayed out even later and went to a club. You would never hear about that, especially not back before everything was on social media. Did it make them more responsible than what Carter did?

He made sure there was a plan to get him to the ceremony and back without disrupting any of his game-day routines, and it was a personal decision that meant a lot to him and his family. He made it back in time, didn't miss a thing, and was ready to play.

I didn't get worked up about it, and you probably wouldn't have either if it hadn't just happened to land on the day of the biggest game in Raptors history.

Carter didn't have his best game that day. He shot 6-for-18 from the field. But he battled through a poor shooting game, got to the free-throw line nine times, and with two seconds left in the fourth quarter, the Raptors had the ball, and trailing 88–87, had a chance to win the game.

Everyone in the building knew who was getting the ball. If you're a Raptors fan, you probably remember what happened next. Dell Curry inbounded the ball to Carter, who ran to the corner, pump faked, got off a shot at the buzzer.

The building held its breath. One team would be going home. The other would advance to the Eastern Conference finals. It all hinged on this one shot.

I was sitting courtside at the time, and from my view, the shot looked good. I was sure it was going in. It hit the rim and bounced off, and the sold-out Sixers crowd exhaled and cheered in unison.

Immediately, everyone on media row buried our heads to write our game stories. I walked to the locker room afterwards and it was pure silence. You could hear a pin drop in there. The players were stunned. They were disappointed. It had been an exhausting playoff run. Nobody knew what to say. Just like that, their season was over.

"It wasn't a play call," Carter said. "It was something [Lenny Wilkens] drew up. Originally on the play, I was supposed to get the ball at the top of the key. But Tyrone Hill was facing me and he kind of jumped to deny, and that's why I jumped and went to the corner. Originally, [it was] up top. I would have space to go one way or another."

Sometimes sports is really simple, no matter how many ways we try to analyze it.

The Raptors got the ball in the hands of their best player on the final possession of the game.

He got a pretty good look.

It just didn't go in.

Sometimes that's just basketball.

I know that a few players thought Carter shouldn't have gone to the graduation, but none of them blamed the trip for him missing the potential series-clinching shot. There was no lingering bitterness about his decision to attend the ceremony that day.

But the lingering impact on the franchise's trajectory because of that one shot? It's hard to ignore. I was convinced, and many people were, that if the Raptors had advanced that season, they would have beaten the Milwaukee Bucks. The Raptors would have played in the NBA finals against Shaquille O'Neal, Kobe Bryant, and the Los Angeles Lakers.

They likely wouldn't have won. That Lakers team was an all-time great team, especially in the post-season, when they went 16–1 and cruised to the title.

The Raptors would have finished runner-up, but a finals appearance would have changed so much for this franchise. They would have surely, with Carter entering his prime, been a much more enticing destination for free agents.

And if the Raptors had made the finals and gotten a superstar in free agency to pair with Carter, he wouldn't have gotten traded to the New Jersey Nets. He might still be wearing a Raptors jersey today. It would have changed the trajectory of the franchise for the next decade, if not more.

Instead, that second-round series ended up being the apex of the Vince Carter era. They never got past the first round with him. A few years later he was gone, and Toronto was in full rebuild mode.

That's sports.

One shot can change everything.

Eighteen years later, almost the exact same scenario. In the 2019 playoffs, the Raptors and Sixers faced off in the second round and once again the series went to a Game 7. This time, the Raptors had home court advantage and liked their chances at home, especially with Kawhi Leonard, one of the most reliable playoff performers in the game.

It was a tense, back-and-forth Game 7. Nobody played particularly well. Not even Leonard, who needed 39 shots that day to score 41 points. The Raptors needed every one of those shots. Nobody wanted to step up on offence, so Leonard shouldered the burden.

The Raptors held the lead for most of the fourth quarter, but Jimmy Butler raced the length of the court after a missed free throw and converted a layup with 4.2 seconds left in the game to tie it up.

90–90.

Raptors ball.

Once again, one shot to win the series.

Once again, everyone in the building knew who the ball was going to.

Most of us knew the play, too. The Raptors had run it plenty of times that season. Leonard was going to get the ball on the inbound, dribble right, and pick a spot to get a shot off.

"That's our play, we call it 'four,'" Nick Nurse said. "We ran it dozens of times [and it] was the only thing we were gonna run. We clear out that side, and swing one guy off, and then swing him looping back around, and then he's got the chance to shoot it off the catch or go on the right side dribble."

Leonard caught the ball, ran towards the corner, right in front of the Raptors' bench, and got a high-arching shot off right before the buzzer sounded, over the outstretched hands of Joel Embiid.

The intensity in the building that day was something I had never felt before, in all the years of covering the team. Everyone knew the stakes. The Leonard trade was made for moments like this. A second-round exit would have been a colossal disappointment.

It was, once again, the most important game in franchise history.

Sitting on media row, I once again had a perfect angle to watch the shot.

When it left his hand, the buzzer sounded, and the balance of two teams' championship hopes hung on which way the ball would bounce.

Nobody could have predicted what came next.

The ball hit the rim and bounced up. Everyone in the arena, along with everyone watching outside in Jurassic Park and across the country, held their collective breath.

A second bounce on the rim, and suddenly, it seemed like maybe, just maybe, this sucker had a chance.

A third bounce.

Holy shit.

On the fourth bounce, the ball seemed to rest gently on the basket.

A moment frozen in time.

The first Game 7 series-clinching buzzer beater in NBA history.

Pandemonium.

"I told him to bounce it three times on the rim," Nurse joked afterwards. "Not four."

My immediate reaction: disbelief.

Nobody could have dreamt of this playing in their backyard growing up.

A four-bounce shot to win a playoff series.

In a Game 7.

Unbelievable.

My second thought?

Man, it looked just like the shot Carter took 18 years earlier.

The parallel of the two shots was incredible.

I talked to Carter about it recently and he agrees.

"It was amazing to see," Carter said. "It was, you look at it and you just turn it over and flip it on the side, here's what this would look like. That's basketball."

That's basketball.

No better way to put it.

That's the absolute beauty of sports.

One shot goes in.

One doesn't.

One brought absolute joy.

One brought absolute dejection.

Sometimes you can do everything to prepare for that moment. You can spend years honing your craft, working on every single shot, preparing for that moment when you can be the hero, but when that ball goes up, you're at the whims of the basketball gods.

People like to debate the end-of-game play calls that are always open to second-guessing, and of course, shots like Carter's and Leonard's in Game 7 will be replayed and talked about from now until eternity. A lot of times, whether it is a good play or not just depends on whether the ball goes in the net when the buzzer sounds.

I didn't see the photos of Leonard's shot until later that evening. You could see it on all the players' faces. On the Raptors and Sixers. They were all in disbelief. They didn't know what to do. Nobody had ever seen anything like that before. And it was true. It was the first time a Game 7 ended on a buzzer beater.

The picture of Leonard's shot is going to go down as one of the best sports photos in Canadian sports history. It's not even the same sport, but I think it's up there with Paul Henderson's game-winning goal in the 1972 Summit Series, and probably even bigger than when Donovan Bailey won the 100-metre Olympic Gold Medal at the 1996 Summer Olympics in Atlanta.

Just like Carter's shot, what Leonard did changed the trajectory of this franchise. Without it, they'd have lost again in the second round, and the one-year experiment with Leonard would be considered a failure by a lot of people. I would still argue that it was a no-brainer trade for Masai Ujiri. And if they went for it and didn't get the ultimate prize, you couldn't blame him for going for it in the first place. You take your shot when you think you have a chance.

Without the shot, there would be no championship, no parade, no legacies for all these players on the Raptors who will forever be celebrated in this city. It would have changed the summer, too. Kyle Lowry probably wouldn't have returned. He definitely wouldn't have signed an extension. It's likely Ujiri would have explored trade options for Serge Ibaka and Marc Gasol, and hastened the entire process of turning the page on this roster.

Instead, the Raptors are defending champions.

That's how fragile sports is.

Two shots.

Two different outcomes.

25

CHAMPIONSHIP NIGHT

The meeting room of the luxurious St. Regis Hotel in the SoMa district of San Francisco had been turned into a video theatre on the morning of June 13, 2019. Chairs aligned just so, a giant screen for all to look at. It could have been any meeting of any group of any middle managers of any company on earth as the participants began to straggle in that morning.

But these were not suit-clad executives on some training seminar they could sleep through; they had lessons to learn that a mere 12 hours later would change their lives forever, and the mood was not full of cheer and goodwill and maximizing the profits in the next quarter.

These were the Toronto Raptors, on the verge of making basketball history, and as they gathered that Thursday morning, it was not in celebration and the mood was not all sweetness and light.

Coach Nick Nurse stood before them that morning before Game 6 of the NBA finals and basically read them the riot act. There was no cheerleading, no massaging of egos or telling them what they wanted to hear.

A historic day began with harsh words.

"We had a morning film session that was fairly lengthy, and fairly, well, on the rougher side," was how Nick Nurse remembered that fateful morning.

The Raptors led the best-of-seven championship series 3–2 at that point and needed just one more victory to earn the first NBA title for a non–United States team in NBA history. They had squandered an opportunity to close out the series three nights earlier in Toronto, and the mistakes—tiny blown assignments that are so critical against an opponent as good as the Golden State Warriors, who were the two-time defending NBA champions—could not be repeated.

The Raptors had been up six points with about three minutes left in Game 5 at home and you could smell the storybook finish. League officials were preparing the back of house for the celebration, the Larry O'Brien Trophy was in the building, and the arena, the city, the country were ready to explode. I remember thinking it was almost too good to be true, that this couldn't possibly happen because it was too well scripted. And then it didn't, and I could imagine how many people were scared or nervous; the sense of trepidation was real as we all got ready for another cross-continent flight.

Lesser teams may have rested on their laurels, felt supremely confident being so close to the ultimate goal. Nurse would not allow it. "There are just some things, some mistakes we couldn't make. I was showing some things, I was adamant that this can't happen. We can't gamble and lunge in the backcourt, we can't go to the offensive glass if we don't have a chance to get it.

"That night was the night we had to do all that stuff and throw all that stuff away and be sound for 48 minutes. No gambling.

"I remember having a big speech out—'You guys ever been to Vegas? That's why those big casinos are there, because of the gamblers who lost. We need to stop gambling on everything.'"

The mood was a bit different just a few blocks away at the media hotel, where we all awoke imagining what the day might bring. I'd covered about 18 NBA finals before this one, had seen dramatic seventh game closeouts like Miami over San Antonio, San Antonio over Detroit. I'd watched Boston and the Lakers in epic duels, and five of the six Chicago Bulls championships. I was in the arena in Miami in 2013 when Ray Allen prolonged a series against the San Antonio Spurs—off a great pass and offensive rebound from Chris Bosh against a team that included Kawhi Leonard and Danny Green. I was in the Delta Center in Salt Lake City when Michael Jordan hit a championship shot for the Chicago Bulls after pushing off Bryon Russell of the Utah Jazz. But none of those moments, as historic as they were, involved *my* team, and the day was nerve-racking because I was so close to it.

Nothing even came close to the nerves, the anticipation and, yeah, the trepidation I felt. We all felt. What kind of opening paragraphs would we write, how could we describe a moment in Canadian sports history like the one we might see? How would we possibly feel if the unthinkable happened? I found myself at times drifting to the bad old days, the 16-win third season, all those lost years when we started charting the draft lottery in February and that was the highlight of the last half of the season. All those players with marginal talent who'd come and gone, all the very good players who were never surrounded with enough talent to be true contenders; so much bad history.

The game was almost a blur.

Kyle Lowry off to a blazing start with 11 straight points to start the game. Klay Thompson was injured early, which robbed Golden State of another star after they'd already lost Kevin Durant to a torn Achilles in Game 5.

And Fred VanVleet.

The "Bet on Yourself" kid, the undrafted, unheralded backup who had 12 points in that magical fourth quarter of Game 6—three three-pointers and three foul shots—to steal some of the spotlight away from the likes of Lowry, Leonard, Marc Gasol, and Pascal Siakam.

About 12 hours after the day began with so many nerves, standing in a corner of the Raptors locker room at the Oracle Arena in Oakland, watching as the players and coaches and medical staff and training staff and support staff cavorted in a champagne-soaked celebration that was loud and joyous and out of control with players pouring bottles of champagne and cans of beer over their own heads and spraying anyone within spitting distance because that's what champions do, we were exhausted.

And euphoric.

I'd written what, in hindsight, was an average opening paragraph, I thought:

OAKLAND, CALIF.—From the cartoonish little dinosaur and gaudy pinstriped jerseys to world champions, a phenomenal quarter-century run ended in joyous celebration for the Toronto Raptors.

What it should have been was my first instinct:

OAKLAND, CALIF.—Dinosaurs rule the world again.

In any case, there we were, standing with team president Masai Ujiri as he surveyed the scene from a safe distance.

None of us knew at that point about his tussle with the off-duty cop that put at least a bit of a damper on his joy. The cop had tried to deny him access to the court to join the wild, impromptu celebrations, and there'd been some kind of physical confrontation. Ujiri was okay, just a bit ruffled but not all out of sorts.

Sort of like us.

In the after-buzzer craziness, when the entire arena was trying to comprehend that the Raptors had beaten the mighty Warriors and won the NBA title, a handful of us, Lori Ewing of the Canadian Press, Mike Ganter of the *Toronto Sun*, got caught up in a wave of fans streaming down the back stairs and somehow got lost, ending up outside the arena. We found a sympathetic cop—not an easy thing because they were all ushering people away from the building and trying to make sure no one got unruly—who got us turned around and into a back hallway that somehow led to the work area adjacent to the interview room and the Raptors locker room.

We'd missed one full interview session with Nick Nurse, and barely caught Fred VanVleet's appearance, but our biggest fear had been that we'd be swept up in the disappointed crowd still trying to get out of the arena and not be able to see the bulk of the celebration.

Imagine that. Missing the greatest celebration in franchise history because we'd taken the wrong stairs? Thankfully, the cop who spotted our credentials and actually listened to our story got us into the right door.

Then it was off to the locker room, where friendly NBA media relations officials recognized us and ushered us in. It was madness. Champagne and beer flew everywhere, players wore goggles so they could see to douse each other, it was madness a degree I'd never seen. At all those other NBA finals, I was a dispassionate observer and seldom ventured into the post-championship locker room. That was for team people and the regular writers; I had stories to file that didn't need the ultimate colour or atmosphere, and besides, who wanted to get soaked with champagne from a celebration of a team that you had no connection to?

This? This was different. These were my guys, my friends, guys I'd written about and talked to for years. Miss this? You got to be kidding me.

And standing there, with Masai, and with Wayne Embry, who had a seat just far enough away to be safe from the champagne and beer but close enough to feel the celebration, was special and not to be missed.

It was a scene we'd never imagined. Crazy happy players dousing themselves and each other with cheap champagne and even cheaper beer, sloshing to and fro with no regard for decorum; plastic sheets covering lockers and the floor and insanity everywhere.

We did our journalism thing—taping a quick conversation with Masai and Wayne so there'd be a live quote to dump into the later stories—but mostly it was watching and smiling and seeing friends happier than they'd ever been.

Ujiri was beside himself. He knew of the morning meeting, he understood a coach's demand that no one settle for anything less than perfection, and after watching the team perform almost perfectly and after watching Nurse, the unproven NBA coach in whom Ujiri had placed so much responsibility, demand excellence and get it, Ujiri could hardly contain his glee.

"I told you we would win in Toronto. I knew we would win in

Toronto," he said to a group of reporters trying to avoid the showers of champagne and beer.

"I told you. And we did it."

That night, that day, was the culmination of a 10-week run that was exhilarating, exhausting, emotional, and a once-in-a-lifetime experience. Standing in that locker room, seeing unbridled joy, hearing shouts and screams and indecipherable noises of excitement, was truly something else. I'd seen athletes celebrate before—I'd covered the 1992 and 1993 Blue Jays and been in the World Series clubhouses after wins—but this was different.

These were my guys. My franchise. My history.

And to have been on that ride was something else.

It was like being outside yourself. We were away from the height of the celebration, in a corner of a large locker room standing with Masai Ujiri and Bobby Webster and Wayne Embry, the giant of a man who sat in a chair like the wonderful overseer he is, soaking it all in. The noise, screams of joy, the fizz of beer cans and champagne bottles being popped is something I'll never forget, nor will anyone who was in that room.

There were many magical moments on Toronto's 10-week-long playoff run in 2019, moments that will be etched in franchise lore forever, and to have lived them up close was emotional and fun and filled with enough "Holy crap!" moments to last a lifetime.

The night of Game 4 in Philadelphia in the second round was a portend of the emotion, the drama, the thrills to come, and it set the stage for two series that followed.

The Raptors trailed that best-of-seven series 2–1 and had been clubbed by 20 points three nights earlier. The Sixers, a cocky group when they played at home, demonstrative and boosted by a loud and raucous crowd, could take ultimate control of the series with a win and we all knew it.

It was that night, late in that vital game, that we found out just how cold-blooded, how calm in the face of disaster Kawhi Leonard could be. And it started a process of discovery that was amazing for those who watched closely. We had always heard about the very best players having an extra gear for the playoffs, something in reserve mentally and physically that allowed them to be even greater when the stakes were highest.

Leonard began to show us that night just what that meant and just what he was, and it was astonishing.

Late in that game in Philadelphia, a tight, predictably intense play-off game that could turn a series, Leonard made a huge three-point shot—from the right wing and right in the face of a defender—that made our jaws drop. It was simply an "Eff you" shot, taken with full confidence in an unspeakable cauldron of pressure on the road against a very good team, and sitting a few rows up in the baseline media seats, I remember thinking: "This guy's got stones."

We had seen big shots and big plays in regular-season games here and there and that was all well and good, but this was under incredible, pressure-filled circumstances, and I thought for the first time that, okay, this guy is special, this team is special, this might be some kind of run.

We couldn't have imagined what was to come to set up that Game 6 euphoria in Oakland.

I don't know what it's ultimately going to be called decades from now when Raptors fans are sitting around and remembering the most dramatic and important shot in franchise history.

The Shot?

The Four-Bouncer?

Maybe it's best remembered by my immediate reaction:

Holy shit!

But if there was ever a doubt that Leonard had whatever clutch gene that all great athletes seem to have, or that he could sense a moment like few others, or that the 2019 team seemed destined for complete greatness, the shot that ended that Philadelphia series was as dramatic a play as you could imagine.

Dribbling to his right as the final seconds of Game 7 wound down—a tied game that would ultimately determine which of the Raptors or Sixers would play for the Eastern Conference title, Leonard's shot over seven-foot Joel Embiid, right in front of the Toronto bench while a crowd of more than 20,000 fans held its collective breath, hit the rim four times as the final buzzer sounded and the place exploded and the Raptors won another series.

All I can remember is the wave of sound that came when it went in; it rushed over us like nothing I'd heard before in that arena. We were about 17 rows up in the stands, almost directly in line with the trajectory of the shot, and looking along the row of writers, it was like none of us could believe what we'd just seen.

Total exhilaration on the bench and in the stands, total amazement in the press seats. We had to quickly get composed and try to write a sentence or two for the top of our stories that were due that very second, and that was as hard a job as any I've ever had. Some of us were shaking with disbelief, and you try capturing that drama in a sentence or two while madness abounds.

But all it did was prepare us for more of the same to come, give us practice for what was to come; it was another step on the journey to Game 6 of the NBA finals. The Leonard mythology and the brilliance of that special group were just starting, really.

It was like we were all caught on this magical journey and it was just a matter of going along for the ride. You could sense something special was unfolding, and who knew where it would take us? All I could sense was that it would be like nothing I'd experienced in more than 20 years around this team.

The conference final against Milwaukee, the number-one team in the conference led by the Greek Freak Giannis Antetokounmpo, was another emotional roller coaster of a ride that took us all from devastating lows to incredible highs.

The Raptors lost the first two games in Milwaukee, and I remember thinking that maybe the ride was going to come to an end, that reality would set in and what was a great run would not turn into the ultimate journey.

Game 3 of that series was epic, and continued to illustrate just how special this Raptors team was. Kyle Lowry fouled out with about five minutes left in the fourth quarter, the team's soul and leader taken from it at the moment he was needed the most. Pascal Siakam missed two free throws with about eight seconds left that probably would have sealed the game.

Instead, it was—again—Leonard who had eight points in the second of two overtime periods as Toronto won to, again, save its season.

"It's amazing," Raptor Norman Powell said of Leonard after the game. "He's a guy that all he wants to do is win. He doesn't care about accolades, the points. We feed off of that. He's a great leader for us."

There were other moments in that series. Leonard dunking over Antetokounmpo in the decisive Game 6 just provided another example of his brilliance and sent shudders through all of us. We were seeing individual brilliance under the most intense circumstances imaginable, proof again that the greatest do really rise to the occasion when it is most needed.

We'd seen so many Raptors teams fall short in the past, unable to get over that proverbial hump, that we were almost giddy seeing this group meet every challenge and beat it back.

Game 6, though?

Game 6 was amazing, the biggest hurdle the Raptors had ever faced. Playing the two-time defending champions in their arena, the very last game in the Oracle Arena before the Warriors moved to a new palace across the bay in San Francisco. A stacked team of proven champions that was not going to go quietly into that good night. The Raptors, the upstart, come-from-nowhere, never-done-anything Raptors, were on the precipice of history. The sense of anticipation was almost too much to handle.

When it was all over, after Fred VanVleet had performed his fourth-quarter heroics, after Kyle Lowry had dominated the start of the game as if to warn the Warriors and their fans that the Raptors truly were for real, as we all stood in the soaking-wet delirium of the team's locker room, watching the celebration rage, it was almost surreal.

The day had begun with some tension and some hard questions asked, hard points made. It ended in pandemonium, with unbridled joy and a scene few of us could have ever imagined.

The Toronto Raptors.

NBA champions.

Dinosaurs ruled the world.

EPILOGUE

On the day of the championship parade, nobody had any idea how it would play out or what the day would hold. We had no clue that over two million people would show up or how it would all work logistically. The Raptors told us that reporters needed to arrive downtown about five in the morning to get their credentials and get settled, and I may be a morning person but that was never going to happen. I'm not big on crowds at the best of times, so spending more time than necessary was not in the cards; I was aiming to arrive at the start of the parade route at eight in the morning.

Arriving at the GO station at seven in the morning, I watched as three trains full of fans heading downtown for the parade passed by. You couldn't move on the platform, and everyone seemed to be wearing some kind of Raptors gear, carrying signs, ready to celebrate like they'd never celebrated before. That was my first inkling that this would be unlike any other championship parade we had ever seen in Toronto, perhaps in the history of North American sports.

I bailed on my trip because I'm a wise old owl and decided to head for my go-to neighbourhood bar in Mississauga to watch the rest of the day's proceedings. It's a decision I don't regret. The parade is a very public event, but I feel like it's a private moment, too. Or at least it was for me. I wasn't going to get accolades; I knew my access to the players, coaches, and officials would be limited at best, and it was their moment. I didn't need to be there to share it.

For the players, it was a time for them to celebrate. They had earned this with a once-in-a-lifetime post-season run. The images of Marc Gasol from the parade will last a lifetime and beyond. You could see the joy on the players' faces as the parade buses rolled through downtown Toronto. Every single street corner was packed. It felt like the celebration would go on forever. Nobody would have objected if it did.

The team had just finished partying with Drake in Las Vegas, but on parade day, they got a second party wind. It was a chance to share the championship with a fan base that had supported them through all the ups and downs.

As the playoffs went along, the players on the Raptors really started to realize that they weren't just playing for themselves, or the city of Toronto. They were playing for an entire country. Players always paid lip service to the whole "playing for Canada" thing, but I think they really felt it during the championship run.

After 24 years covering the team, it was a day to sit back, reflect, and enjoy the moment. It was nice to watch from afar. I was glad I wasn't there in the madness with all the crowds. You cover the team, you get to know the players, you form relationships with people in the organization. You're so close to it, but you're not in it. That was the feeling of parade day for me. It was fun to just sit back and watch the players enjoy it all.

I couldn't help but feel a sense of accomplishment, too, having told the stories about this team through all the years. From the very first game. From Damon Stoudamire, to Vince Carter, to Chris Bosh, to Kyle Lowry and DeMar DeRozan, and now Kawhi Leonard.

When the Raptors finally made it to Nathan Phillips Square, it felt like the day still needed a signature moment. It was fitting who would provide it with a perfect closing image of the championship parade.

Kawhi Leonard took the mic, hesitantly because that's who he is, and addressed the fan base. It felt like the first time the two sides really connected on this deep, personal level. All season, the fan base had cheered and supported him from afar, and now was the chance for Leonard to show his appreciation to the city that yearned for him to stay, to make this championship parade an annual thing.

A few weeks later, Leonard would make his decision in free agency and sign with the Los Angeles Clippers, but nothing on this day could dampen the fans' excitement.

And of course, like he did throughout the playoffs, Leonard came through in the clutch. He closed his speech with an imitation of the same laugh he gave us on media day when we first met him, followed by a mic drop. Everyone on stage, the players, coaches, Masai Ujiri, nearly fell out of their seats.

It was the perfect final scene of an incredible season.

The Raptors finally had the last laugh.

ACKNOWLEDGMENTS

There are too many people who are owed such great debts of thanks that I apologize right off the bat to those who I've missed.

Huge thanks to Nick Garrison and Alanna McMullen, and all the many folks at Penguin Random House who nurtured a neophyte through an unfamiliar process.

To all the Raptors players, coaches, managers, support staff, friends, and colleagues who provided a lifetime of memories and fun and, yeah, some trying times—all of which led us to this point.

To John Lashway, Jim LaBumbard, Jennifer Quinn, and all their media relations staffers for help, guidance, and a wonderful work environment since 1995.

To the many, many gifted colleagues and bosses at *The Star* who gave me my head and let me run with a beat that became a life, starting with the great Chris Young, who encouraged me to get on board.

And to Alex Wong, a colleague and friend without whose support and skill this book would be filled with empty pages.

INDEX